Meeta's Memoirs

Meeta Piatkowska

With love
Meeta Piatkoska

PublishAmerica
Baltimore

© 2006 by Meeta Piatkowska.

All rights reserved. No part of this book may be reproduced, stored in a retrieval system or transmitted in any form or by any means without the prior written permission of the publishers, except by a reviewer who may quote brief passages in a review to be printed in a newspaper, magazine or journal.

First printing

ISBN: 1-4241-1350-4
PUBLISHED BY PUBLISHAMERICA, LLLP
www.publishamerica.com
Baltimore

Printed in the United States of America

Dedicated to my sons and daughters-in-law

Marek and Jackie
Stephen and Gillian

and
my friend Sandra

1

August 13, 2002

I'm sitting on my swing, looking up at the jagged spaces of bright sky through the apple tree and thinking of my future. Some might say this is ridiculous at my age, but I certainly don't think so. I feel an excitement, a breathlessness for what's in store (probably a heart attack!). Up to now, according to others, my life has been fraught with unending adventures of interest. How many times I have been told to write it all down—but this is not easy. Yesterday I tried. Sitting in my lovely arbour in my secret garden with my glass of Chablis and far more than Jane Austen ever had to inspire her. I sat with pen poised and with stories to write that the masters would have died for. Hours passed but the page remained blank. It just shows that if one's a genius, one can write about nothing, whereas I, with mountains of material, cannot give the pen any messages at all. But I'm not one to give up, so at the age of seventy-eight, here goes. Time cannot wait any longer. Where do I start on this soul-searching journey? I suppose at the beginning. Fasten your safety belts, it gets rough!

Memories are strange things; some wonderful and some quite ordinary moments remain vividly in one's mind while others fade into oblivion. I recall at the age of fourteen lying on a rug on our lawn thinking, *Out of interest, let me hold this moment forever.* What made me do this? I don't know, except perhaps the feeling of vast eternal space above urged me to try and retain the moment just as it was. Here I am, sixty-three years later, and the experiment worked. I close my eyes and I'm transported back to that exact time: the scents, the hum of the bees, those few magical seconds of a fourteen-year-old. Let's hope I can recall incidents of real interest that I did not try to retain.

It all began September twenty-seventh, nineteen twenty-five. My sister Maureen, who was four, was taken into the bedroom to see her new sister. Maureen, according to my father, promptly went to the mirror and said, "I'm much nicer." This was probably correct, as newborns are not beautiful, but don't misconstrue her remark; we were, and always will be, very good friends.

We lived in Northenden in a big rather dark old house called Holly Bank in Boat Lane, which led down to the River Mersey. The name Northenden was said to have originated from a certain Earl Nowordine, but I prefer to believe the legend of the smugglers who came up the river calling it their northern den (this is the nearest I shall get to a possible untruth in the following story). It was a small, picturesque village abounding with personalities, odd and interesting characters, and situations fraught with melodrama and intrigue. There were also the necessary shops: butcher, baker, sweet shop and smithy, etc., all important kings and queens ruling over their small domains, not like today, when there's four of everything, all doing badly and falling under the heavy boot of the supermarkets. And the produce! One didn't dare complain about the goose from Mrs. Worsnop's or the bread from the baker, who always looked as if he had fallen in the flour bin. Oh, no! You dare not complain, but on the other hand you never needed to. They took such pride in their wares. It was good, very good.

In the centre of the village was what we called the croft, a large expanse of bare ground that was used by the fair at holiday time, but when vacant was used as a playground by local boys. Our garden wall backed onto it, and I could sit on an oak tree branch that overhung the wall and look onto the croft. Also backing onto the croft was a row of tiny cottages, in one of which lived my first love, Tom Power, and his wife and nine children. Tom was the most wonderful-looking man: tall with very thick, curly black hair and a strong Irish accent. He had a bad reputation in the village for drinking, fighting, and being a terror with women. Later I realized that a lot of this was village gossip, but a little truth too. Women were immensely susceptible to his charm and good looks, and I was no exception, but I was only six years old. He did many odd jobs, our garden being one of them. Actually like men do today he spent most time looking after his children while his wife, a clever qualified nurse, worked night shifts.

On my frequent unauthorized visits to the Power family's cottage in late evening I loved to watch Tom in charge. I always managed to escape from the inexperienced young nursemaid, who would never have dared tell my parents anyway. There seemed to be only one big room downstairs (there probably was a small parlour, but I never saw that). This room rather like a large kitchen with a stone floor, no carpet, and a huge fire burning in a great iron range. There was a large oven on the right and on the top would be a vast pan that Tom would stir and taste occasionally.

On the floor in front of the fire would be a tin bath full of steaming water, where little Powers would be bathed two at a time by the older children. A long wooden table would be set with spoons and a large plate piled high with delicious bread from the white baker. Eventually all the Powers would sit with rosy faces around the table, including me, with spoons at the ready. Tom would ladle out the steaming food, which always tasted wonderful. Possibly Mrs. Power, working night shifts while her husband stayed at home, was considered wrong in nineteen thirty-one, but I knew Tom was an adored and kind father.

As the years passed I heard the children did well, and Tom lived happily to an old age in a cottage in Styal, Cheshire. I met him again after forty years and learnt there had been something between us—but patience, that comes later!

My family on both sides could certainly take their places top of the list as being odd and interesting. My mother was five feet eleven and extremely beautiful and talented. To name just a few of her accomplishments: she could paint and was a friend and artist with Graham Sutherland; at the age of sixteen she became a designer for Courtalds; she was an excellent pianist, playing anything put before her from Beethoven to Chopin; she sang on the BBC; she was one of six glamorous models who freelanced modelling beautiful dresses for the best gown shops, a bit like the fashion models today. One week the fashion house wanted a child so I modelled at the age of five. But there was a flaw in this brilliant woman's personality: she very quickly became bored. As soon as she achieved something, she wanted to try something else. Sadly I think my sister and I were like her many projects, and were soon handed over to very young and inexperienced nannies with disastrous results, luckily none fatal.

Maureen fell out of her pram, lost the end of her finger and contracted peritonitis at the age of two, which sadly prevented her having children; and she also cut her bottom rather badly on an outside broken lavatory. I, too, was in and out of trouble, but of a different sort than my sister. Where she was a good little girl, I was inclined to be rather naughty, rebellious and venturesome, so besides my quota of cuts and stitches, I also got up to all sorts of mischief.

My father was small, approximately five feet five, had extremely poor sight, and wore very thick glasses, but he made up for this a thousand times by being the most likeable character anyone could meet. We possessed two such people in our family, wonderful people whom everyone liked, never-to-be forgotten people: one was my father, the other was my grandmother on my mother's side, Carrie (Hillkirk) Alderley, daughter of the infamous Major Jock Hillkirk, my great-grandfather. I'm coming to him later! As I was saying, my father was well-liked by everyone; his success was his kindness, his great sense of humour, and a beautiful speaking voice that he could render in six languages. I don't think his childhood had been too happy. He lived in luxury in Egypt with his parents, one brother and two sisters. Their father was British and their mother was French. At the age of nine he was sent to England to Stony Hurst College, was put in the charge of a guardian and never returned to his family. When he finished his studies he became an apprentice at the Royal Cotton Exchange Manchester, where he became quite a well-known figure. In the early days he worked hard and things were going quite well. He and my mother, whom he adored, settled at Holly Bank. They even acquired a live-in maid, though rather sooner than was intended.

May arrived on our doorstep at midnight. She was sixteen, crying, and pleading for us to employ her. It seems that she worked for the local doctor, whose wife was incredibly mean, and poor May was starving. I believe my father said that his finances did not yet stretch to a uniformed maid, but May implored him, saying, "I don't care. You don't need to pay me, but I will not go back to that awful woman!" May did stay till she married; she never lost touch with us, dying in her eighties.

We did not own Holly Bank. It belonged to my mother's parents, who during their prosperous years owned most of Northenden. Gradually the wealth had disappeared, which was the sad thing about both families: they lost vast amounts of money for different reasons. On my mother's side we had Major Jock Hillkirk, and on my father's political trouble with the cotton industry.

To start with Daddy was hard-working, gradually doing better every year, although I don't think things were easy. Both my parents loved parties and had lots of friends, and I think we always lived a little beyond our finances; they were always either entertaining or dressing up to go out. Mummy would look absolutely stunning in fantastic creations. Two dresses remain in my mind: one figure-hugging black chiffon down to her ankles, with four bands of rhinestones winding around her, each ending in a large rhinestone tassel on her left side as they spiralled down her beautiful figure; the other soft chiffon in shades of grey embossed with velvet, the hem all different points and layers. My small father would proudly escort his glamorous Kate, himself looking smart in a dinner suit with a crimson cummerbund.

When there was a lull in the excitement, my mother would become bored and retire to bed saying she was ill—until, of course, a party became imminent, when she would miraculously recover and appear a vision of beauty. During these lapses my father would hire a housekeeper. We got through a strange motley of these ladies. One, a most efficient woman, had a glass eye that she placed in a tumbler at night, which intrigued me. There was one other problem: being so efficient, she saved money on food, so we were always hungry. Daddy would creep into the nursery with food. We were all scared of her, even Daddy, but Mummy was never scared of anything or anybody.

As I said before, housekeepers and nannies came and went, but May and Mrs. Grout were permanent. Mrs. Grout, what a character! One could write a whole book about her. She came in daily to clean, always keeping her duster tucked in her bosom. I did wonder whether it was there all the time. She would tell me wonderful stories; my limited education was increased enormously by her revelations. She had been abroad with her husband while he was a soldier; he had gone mad with religious mania and it took her many years to get him released from the asylum. Her stories were always told with lurid descriptions, facial distortions and arm waving; in fact, she was a great storyteller, keeping me at the tender age of around seven completely enthralled. She knew a great deal about Northenden, especially my grandfather the major. In fact at the top of Boat Lane was Church Street with a row of small cottages, in one of which lived Aunt Jess (no relation, that's just what she was called). She ran a brothel in her cottage. Major Hillkirk was a frequent visitor. Once, at one of Aunt Jess's infamous parties, according to Mrs. Grout they had a competition as to which of the young ladies had the largest fanny, the local gentlemen doing the judging! I asked with my usual curiosity, "How did they do that?" It seems they sat in a row with knees apart! Can you imagine that small cobbled street, the horses and carriages waiting, the tiny row of cottages all aglow with lamps and candles? I presume they were all involved. I feel compelled to retell these stories of things that happened over a hundred years ago.

Major Jock Hillkirk

Before Aunt Jess retired to take charge of the brothel she gave her last performance. At the age of fifty, she led a procession down Boat Lane, dancing in all-over pink tights and gold and silver spangles, her waist corseted to ridiculously tiny proportions. As Mrs. Grout's voice became more excited, rising to her feet, her arms raised, I could almost see Aunt Jess resplendent and looking similar to the Degas painting of the trapeze artist. Aunt Jess reigned over the street, living past ninety. A certain Lord Chipperfield of the Circus, when performing near, would send his Rolls Royce for her and she would have the best seat in the big top.

Another Grout story was about Kruger. Kruger was the butler to a gentleman who lived in a large square house in Royal Green Road. This was a continuation of Church Road, which ran at the top of the infamous Church Street. One night Kruger shot his master. It became a siege with the police surrounding the house. Eventually Kruger was well and truly killed, shot many times, and his body was deposited in the mortuary, which happened to be in Church Road. Later that night some of the villagers got rather drunk, and being very fond of the man Kruger had murdered, decided he hadn't been punished enough, so they stole his body from the mortuary and brought him down Boat Lane, carrying him shoulder-high, intending to throw him in the River Mersey. By this time Kruger was rather stiff. Suddenly for some reason they took fright and hurriedly propped him upright in our hedge and ran off. Later a courting couple stopped to kiss and came face to face with a white-faced Kruger!

There were good moments, particularly Christmas. I loved Christmas and still do. The first one that comes to mind, I was in one of my favourite places. The black welsh dresser had a space in the middle between the cupboards on either side and I could hide in it. There I could survey the large kitchen. From where I watched it seemed huge, rather like the giant's kitchen in "Jack and the Beanstalk." On one wall there was a row of bells with the numbers of the rooms above them. They had long been out of use but sometimes I imagined (or did I?) that they quivered and one gave a dull ring! I loved watching from my hidey hole the hustle and bustle on Christmas Eve, and smelling wonderful aromas of spices, herbs, oranges, lemons, cloves and holly! The gas light gave off a mysterious glow, always leaving dark corners unlit, not like electricity, which reveals every nook and cranny with its stark glare. The main attraction was the large iron range highly polished with black lead, surrounded by a tall black fender topped with shiny brass, I suppose to keep me safe from the blazing fire in the centre.

Hearing excited voices coming from the hall (my father and Uncle Ted had arrived), I crawled from my hiding place in time to see the green tip of the Christmas tree appearing through the front door. With much struggling, arguing, and laughter, gradually the tip became longer and longer, wider and wider, until the full length and width of the hall was filled with tree. "It's far too big as usual!" my mother exclaimed as she stood on the stairs, but they got the tree installed eventually in the bay window in the lounge where it loomed high and dark! We all celebrated this achievement with glasses of ginger wine all round.

Then came the decorating. A ladder was brought and a box of decorations. What exciting things that box contained. There were cries of "Oh! Look at this. How pretty! Where's the fairy? Let's have the star this time. Oh, look at that. Do you remember this?" And then dozens of coloured tin clip-on candle holders with twisty candles, all to be lit by hand! Now this is where my mother came to the fore. "Where shall we put this, Kate?" "Is that right, Kate?" "And where shall we hang the bells?" My mother always knew. "A little more to the right. No! No! George, get the ladder, for goodness sake! That's not right, it's upside down. Oh! George, give it to me, I can reach without the ladder. Now get the ladder and put that at the top."

Eventually it was all done, now resplendent, no longer looming tall and dark but all aglitter. Time for bed. Our brown stockings were hung ready for Father Christmas, the gas fire left on low to splutter and hiss, lighting the nursery with a dim glow. When my sister became aware that Father Christmas was Daddy, I also was informed, so the fantasy came to an end rather abruptly.

But I must leave this moment and hasten on with my tale. When the fair came to Northenden I would climb the oak tree and sit on our high wall, dangling my legs and watching all the fun. Just beneath me an old gypsy and his wife always parked their caravan, and next to it was their contribution: an infants' roundabout. It was a tiny replica of the magnificent horses that had pride of place in the centre of the fair; the couple worked it by hand. They invited me into their caravan one day. It was a treasure cave of cut glass mirrors and lustre ornaments. Even I so young could see it was unique.

The fair when it came was a wonderful experience. First came the noise of the steam engines, which once started would throb continuously in the background. This was the heart of the fair, working the machinery; there was always a strong smell of diesel. One soon got drawn into the hubbub of laughter, voices, hurdy-gurdy music, and small stalls, rolling pennies, hoopla and suchlike. Reigning supreme in the centre was the great roundabout with the glorious horses with names to match. We all had our favourites; mine was the black one. Each horse was attached to a huge shiny brass spiral pole; they flew around the truly magnificent organ with its vividly painted figures performing jerkily as the music played. I used to listen to it from my bed. There were stalls selling hot and steamy black puddings and you could watch while the delicious golden ginger snaps were being twirled. Natural sugar cane could also be bought. All mouth-watering! Then there were the mysterious booths with fortune tellers and freaks, and the boxing booth. This is where Tom Power (in his role as the resident boxer) would stand, flexing his muscles and displaying his handsome brown body.

I was invited to the birthday party at Tom Power's cottage. Though there were nine children, they had one party for all. I don't think my mother approved. She knew nothing of my other regular visits, playing on the croft or going to Tom's cottage. Two trestle tables were erected on the croft, their yard being too small. The boys and their friends sat at one, and the girls at the other. I remember not being pleased, as I had been accepted by the boys as one of them. Odd as it may seem I was the only girl in the gang and also the youngest, as the ages ranged from nine to twelve. I was six! My pal was the twelve-year-old Lawrence. My mother would have been horrified, but the boys looked after me. We used to race about the croft on homemade go-carts, wonderful contraptions. Of course I was never allowed to steer one but I had the important job of sitting on the back of Lawrence's vehicle and working the wooden brake when told. I often touched the ground with my bottom, mystifying the poor young nursemaid with my constant torn and black knickers!

After the birthday tea was finished Tom had arranged for us all to go to The Bug Hut. Imagine my excitement, my first visit to the cinema! And Tom, my hero, my love, was the instigator of this wonderful experience! Situated in the centre of the village was the village's pride and joy, The Coronation Cinema. This was situated conveniently next to The Farmer's Arms, both owned by Peter Leigh. The Bug Hut had only just converted to sound but the piano was still played when the occasional silent film was shown.

The Bug Hut was a little behind the times but it had many advantages, such as that while queuing one could have a drink from the pub. The projectionist, Peter Leigh himself, would stand at the top of some steps on the outside of the cinema that led to the projectionist's room. From there he would give us a talk on the wonders we were about to see, and also of the future programmes. We get the same now, only on a big screen.

As we queued Peter Leigh gave his usual talk on his steps, and when he disappeared this was the signal for the ticket lady to appear at a small window, and the doors opened. As we entered the tiny cinema there was a hush and we were met by a thick mixture of cigar smoke, gas and alcohol, all extremely intoxicating to a child. The room was dimly lit by flickering gas lights with red glass shades. The whole place was like a warm red velvet glove with its crimson walls, carpet and seats. I vaguely recollect ornate plaster figures and pillars around the screen. The plush seats were high, up level with my shoulder, but those were the dear seats. We marched down to the front where there were two rows of wooden benches. They were so near my neck ached with looking up at the screen; in fact I did fall over backwards at one point, but soon got used to it. On the back row there were special double seats for lovers; I knew this because one boy at school was very fat and he had to have a double seat to himself. The heavy velvet curtains slowly shushed open and the white screen flickered, the camera whirred, and we were away into the land of cowboys and Indians. I soon learnt that when the film started we all clapped and cheered, but when anything went wrong, which was frequent, we all booed! Occasionally they still showed silent films, which were great fun as then there was real audience participation.

Perhaps it would be appropriate to give a mention to Auntie Peggy, my mother's sister, just as weird and eccentric as the rest of my family. Carrie Alderley was proud of her daughters, and she had good reason to be. Both were unusually bright, and Peggy was exceptionally pretty where my mother Kate was gloriously beautiful. They were both educated at the local council school, Bazley Road. This, I'm sure, was rather a come-down for the Alderleys, but Bazley Road was no ordinary run-of-the-mill school; it turned out many clever and interesting people, and I believe it still continues to do so.

My grandparents, Carrie Hillkirk and Peter William Alderley, went against their parents' wishes when they married. According to Grandpa Alderley, he fell in love with Carrie when she was twelve and he was about twenty-two, but they were made to wait until Carrie was twenty-five. Their families were so annoyed that they supplied these two with Kenworthy Farm, Kenworthy Lane, and no money. They just left them to get on with it. This, as you can imagine, was a catastrophe waiting to happen. Neither was used to farming. My grandmother had been used to a young lady's upbringing, a life of gentility, but she was neither lazy nor stupid and she buckled to and coped. To do them justice they did manage for at least fourteen years, but they both had the same weakness for enjoying themselves beyond their means, so the fields would be flooded so skating parties could be enjoyed by all, and eventually the farm went bankrupt and they ended up in a terraced house in the centre of the village, Palatine Road. Poor Carrie, but they at least retained a maid! The strange thing was their friends never deserted them; they were always looked up to, but as I mentioned Carrie was a very unusual woman, loved by everyone. Actually Uncle Ted, who married Peggy, told me that he really wanted her mother. My father also owned up to loving her dearly, and both my sister's husband and mine owned up to such sentiments and would do anything for her. The odd thing was that the women also loved her and accepted the adoration she received as quite normal.

At the terraced house, the two girls had to work. Peggy taught dancing and Kate played the piano for her (my mother says she never got paid), but as always they were both exceptional at their chosen work. As usual the whole family had this addiction to enjoying themselves. Perhaps I ought to clarify this activity: it wasn't sex and drink (this of course excludes Major Jock Hillkirk, who indulged in everything); no, my family's idea of fun was friends, parties, musical evenings, amateur dramatics, any excuse for a gathering of friends, and nearly always held in our own home. This entailed spending money, but at least it was never a selfish kind of enjoyment.

One of these occasions brings Peggy to mind. Peter William and Carrie were entertaining a group of people, which included some of the most influential in the village—the doctor, vicar, etc.—and their wives, all stuffed into my grandparents' lounge. Peggy was going to entertain them with a dance. The floor was cleared and my aunt appeared—browned all over, bare feet, a flower adorning her flowing black hair, and nothing but a sarong swathed about her. Her performances were good, and possibly similar to Isadora Duncan, but halfway through the sarong slipped to her waist and displayed all. Peggy seemed quite oblivious, finished her dance and received her ovation as if nothing had happened.

Peggy also taught ballroom, hiring the Midland Hotel and an orchestra. She made a lot of money but spent it as fast as it came. One of her fortes was doing an exhibition tango with an extremely handsome friend of my father's, Bill Pollard. Once she sewed his velvet trousers up, considering them not tight enough, and when he pleaded to be unstitched for a certain important reason, she indignantly refused to listen. Luckily my father, always being a practical man, helped him in his hour of need, and re-sewed him in time for the performance. During the latter part of the First World War Auntie Peggy used to give the troops shows, and Mummy would play the piano, but one time Peggy insisted (she was very bossy) that Mummy did a Russian Cossack dance. My mother collapsed in the middle of the Russian step and lay unable to move for laughing. The troops laughed too, because all they could see was Mummy's cummerbund rising and falling with her laughter. Auntie Peggy was, as usual, not amused!

Let me spare a few more lines on Peggy. She had a most peculiar nature; my father remarked that she burnt the candle at both ends and in the middle. She wore outrageous outfits. One time at a dance she had on a body-clinging peach satin dress, open-backed to about two inches below the cleavage of her bottom. My father remarked that when he entered the ballroom he thought she had no clothes on.

She had many admirers and danced till all hours. I wonder, have I painted a realistic picture of this extremely pretty, vivacious, quick-tempered, strange girl? Odder still, at the age of about thirty she changed completely, wearing manly, severe clothes, and with a manner to match.

My mother was quite the opposite: beautiful, elegant, no passion at all, naive, completely unaware of her many talents, and too easy-going. She needed entertaining, or boredom set in and off she would go to bed.

Our father often used to make us laugh with his many anecdotes, although he doted on my mother. Behind her back he would remark that even with all her talent she had the brain the size of a pigeon's egg. All their married life she would call him at all hours for tea to be brought to her bed, and one morning when there was snow outside he said, "I think I'll invent a contraption so that when your mother calls, I can press a button which will shoot her out into the snow." Next moment she would call and off he would go.

All the time my parents were at Holly Bank—in fact all their married life—the Thomases, my father's family, came and stayed for months. They arrived from Alexandria, Egypt, en masse by ship. They would bring all sorts of gifts, not small, but furniture and tapestries. There were some articles that stand out in my mind, some exciting and exotic like the wall hanging about two feet by five feet with weird Egyptian figures and hieroglyphics on it; then there were the chairs and settee made of elaborate wooden carving and inlaid with mother of pearl; and best of all the black upright grand piano with its two brass candelabras, which had pride of place in our sitting room and was battered frequently by everyone, particularly at our many parties.

When they arrived we, of course, had to hire more staff and more money was spent, but Daddy's father was not ungenerous while they were with us. The sad part was that when he and his wife died he left nothing to my father. Grandma Meeny was rumoured to be a descendent from Napoleon's court, but to me she was just a rather strange woman, always in black and only able to speak French. She had been beautiful. Grandpa Peeny was still a distinguished man, tall and handsome. Their entourage consisted of their two daughters, May and Bibza, and their younger son Fred, who cut a dashing figure in uniform when a pilot in the First World War.

May was slim, dark, and attractive in a French way. I believe I took after her in looks. She was the type to wear Schaperelli. She later married Col. Phillip Bence-Jones, who it seems was some relative to the Queen Mother. He was a delightful uncle, amiable and easygoing, but Aunty May was inclined to be a snob. She had inherited the Thomases' sense of humour, and one of her tales was how she stood up in the bath naked, the butler walked in and she said, "Oh! Sorry, sir!" This was funny if you compared her tiny slim figure to my huge giant of an uncle.

Daddy's other sister Bibza was a nice jolly girl, with no side at all, and easy to talk to. She also married well; in fact they all were rather wealthy except for us, but what I thought was odd was they never stopped invading us sometimes for weeks in the summer, first at Holly Bank, and then at all the other houses we inhabited.

At Holly Bank, it must have been quite a stressful time for my father, particularly money-wise, but as always his sense of humour prevailed. There was a tiny garret over the front door no bigger than a small toilet, and my father slept there, saying, "I've been evicted to make room for the others."

There certainly was a lot of activity while the family was over. Oh, yes! They also brought their cook Hassien, who for some reason on one occasion went and cooked at the Midland Hotel Manchester. As you can imagine they were used to enormous luxury in Egypt and so my father, trying hard to please, spent a great deal on food and drink, which they all took for granted. I can see now the huge plate piled high with oysters and chunks of lemon being carried into the dining room. But Grandpa Thomas wasn't mean, just completely unaware of Daddy's real situation. According to Mummy he often handed her twenty pounds, which was quite a lot in those days.

When sitting on the floor when I was about three, Grandpa Peeny gave me the elaborate silver sugar basin full of lump sugar. I suppose the reason for this was because they never had to deal with children. I believe Grandma Meeny had a wet nurse for her babies, a woman who breastfed. I cannot imagine anything more disgusting. As soon as their children were about nine years old they were packed off to England to boarding school. As their visits were always in the summer, there was a deal of partying in the garden, which was quite splendid, being tended by my secret love, Tom.

Perhaps as this is my life story I should mention that as far back as I can recall I always had enormous crushes on older men, at least twenty to thirty-five years older. Whether this was normal from three years upwards I've no idea. I was a pretty little girl and I really chased these men when I liked them. They didn't seem to mind. It was not sexual, as the experts would immediately say nowadays; I just adored their company. This behaviour continued even when I was fourteen. Mrs Dean, an old friend of the family who used to play the piano for my classes, often laughingly told the story of how I, when thirteen, knocked on her door and asked if Mr Dean could go to the pictures with me (incidentally he did). I also borrowed Ben Moston's husband. He was such a handsome man. She also played the piano for me sometimes. She was a very clever woman, a poet. She wrote a poem about me that was in *Punch*, but I'm sure I will mention the Mostons again later.

I did borrow quite a few husbands, but the wives never complained. Come to think of it, if any of them had made an improper suggestion I would have been horrified, but of course I knew that would never have occurred. I did like clever people, men or women; perhaps this was something to do with my lack of education?

My sister and I attended a private school run by the worthy Miss Richardson, which was held in a room above the Oddfellows Hall, a small building facing the top of Church Street, only a minute's walk from Holly Bank. Maureen then went on to Withington Girls' Grammar School, but the village doctor said I had something wrong with my heart, so at the age of seven my education came to an abrupt end. My last schoolbook had illustrations and sentences such as "The fat black cat sat on the mat."

And that seemed to be that. I was extremely naughty and possibly Miss Richardson was glad to see the back of me. I know I disrupted the class, spending most of my time either in the corner or on a chair in the middle of the table. This was sad because I really had a great admiration for this woman, who held a class of children aged from five to fourteen—in fact a complete primary school in one room. The children sat at trestle tables according to their ability. She attained exceptional results and many of her pupils becoming leading citizens.

What did I do wrong? According to Auntie Peggy I was quite unteachable. She had attempted to teach me a few steps of dancing when I was five. I was always late for school. As the nanny ran me up the lane we would see Miss Richardson already standing with her back to the window reading the Bible. I would crawl to my seat hoping (without success) that I would be unnoticed. Donovan, a boy who sat near me during sewing class, asked me to help him and by mistake I sewed his tea cloth to my skirt. Another time Miss Richardson took us into the tiny yard for gym. I copied her exercise perfectly, but as she had one very bowed leg, this did not go down well at all! Pity, she never knew what enormous admiration I had for her: her neatness, her gold pence nez on its gold chain, and most of all the way she sharpened my pencil and after every line of l's I would pester her to sharpen it again and again, but when I turned them into fish she didn't seem to appreciate my efforts.

Sometimes I wish I could go back like the old man in the Maupassant story, but not to change my life, just to return for a few moments to say sorry to some people I hurt. There was the instance when my grandmother (Carrie) had lost her beautiful home and what was left of her few treasures in the Blitz. Once again she had returned to a dreadful situation, almost squalor; she was battling bravely as always but I carelessly remarked, "Was it worth going against your parents' wishes and marrying Grandpa?" For the first and last time I saw this deeply courageous woman cry, and it was my stupid ignorance that caused her pain.

Incidentally, her answer was "Yes, oh yes!" Another occasion was when I neglected my sons when they needed me most. I had gone through the mill at the time but that is no excuse; perhaps if this tale is published they will forgive me.

In 1933 we moved house and went to an idyllic cottage, Hollyhocks in Mobberly. We all loved it. I continued to do nothing; Maureen was apprenticed to Cleggs of Wilmslow and she was happy. I gained a rather unusual pet. I had been sent to Antrobus Farm for milk and with the few pence change I bought a tiny yellow chick, which grew into a simply magnificent cockerel. In fact one day a farmer passing offered me three hens for him and was most surprised that this nine-year-old wouldn't take his magnificent offer. Cocky would sit on the top of the piano when my mother was singing and join in with sort of guttural noise, but when she took a high note he would rise up and crow magnificently.

But sadly things seemed to go wrong. Mummy actually became really ill, and I too. Maureen nursed us but eventually we had to go to hospital. During this time Daddy moved us to Hale, a dark three-storied house that he decorated throughout, hoping to please us, but we hated it. The lifestyle did not suit us at all; the atmosphere was much too formal and ordinary. There were rules that neighbours were expected to adhere to: maids had to wear uniform at all times (this upset May), washing should never be seen. Musical soirees were held regularly, but according to Daddy as he donned his dinner suit, "Terribly boring, not to my liking, they are all so miserable!" So we moved in less than six months. Our next port of call was Heald Green, where we spent many happy years. By this time my father's parents had died, leaving absolutely nothing to my father, which seemed odd as he was the eldest. He didn't even receive any of his personal things that he had left in Egypt. I think he was a little hurt but continued to retain his inimitable humour. The rest of his wealthy family continued to come and live with us weeks at a time when it suited them. You can probably guess that I did not approve.

Daddy was doing reasonably well, even gaining quite a reputation as a well-thought-of man on the Royal Cotton Exchange. He loved the place and had an office right at the top of the building. Weatherby, a well-known cartoonist at the time, did a drawing of my father for the *Manchester Evening News*.

By the time I had reached the age of eleven Grandma decided something must be done, so I was taken to a specialist, who found there was nothing wrong with me! Of course it was far too late to send me to school, where I would have stood out like a sore thumb! Luckily, Grandma came up with what seemed the only solution.

She had an old wealthy friend from the past whose daughter wanted to start a dancing school. Granny and Grandpa had inherited a large three-storied house called the Poplars, which backed onto the River Mersey. They also inherited Holly Bank, two rows of cottages in Church Street and Boat Lane, and quite an area of land adjoining the Poplars. One would have presumed they would have been in the money, but this was not the case. Whether this was mismanagement I've no idea.

The long and short of it was that this girl and her friend took over the downstairs floor of the Poplars and my grandparents the two large floors above. These two girls spent a great deal of money turning their part into a luxurious dancing studio with all commodities, which included a huge dance room that could be divided into two classrooms, an office and a kitchen. My grandmother allowed this on condition I became their first pupil, with free tuition to become a teacher (I fear blackmail); this arrangement gave my grandparents a good rent and so everyone was happy.

This all sounds excellent, but there was a slight hitch: the two girls knew nothing about dancing. Granted they had a gift for presentation, showmanship and a great deal of money. They pleased parents with their constant elaborate shows. It's difficult to explain how the school flourished, but it did. Everything was tastefully presented. Smart, expensive green tunics with specially designed badges had to be worn. Ballroom, ballet, Greek dancing, keep fit, competitions and displays all took place, but I knew it was all a great big con, all show and snobbery with no technique.

The two girls soon realized that with my vivid imagination and far-too-grown-up appearance I was quite capable of taking over the infants class, which for them was boring but extremely lucrative. The infants were aged between three and five and they seemed to thoroughly enjoy my arrangements of giants, fairies, trees, flowers and nursery rhymes, so I was exploited regularly, taking classes of easily up to twenty or more when I was just thirteen.

All this time they were struggling to get me through the Royal Academy of Dancing exams from instructions out of a book. They eventually entered me for my first senior exam (still only thirteen) Elementary R.A.D. I suppose this episode would be considered quite funny. I went in with three other candidates. All my exercises were different from theirs; when they were up, I was down; when they were down, guess who was up? They went right, I went left and so on; mind you, I should have been used to being a misfit. Needless to say I did not pass.

One of the oddest lessons was when one of them attempted to teach me acrobatics (from a book). We ended up entangled in knots, she, me and the book of instructions. I noticed at these particular moments of intimacy (if you can call it that) they seemed to get overexcited. I thought their behaviour a little odd but didn't discover the reason till much later. Luckily ignorance is bliss!

They entered me for competitions, surprisingly with real success. At Blackpool I came first in all the four dances, but with my usual luck, instead of being presented with four gold medals, Blackpool had that year decided to economize, so I received a horrible bronze thing with four bars attached. As the girls wanted to improve the image of their school they were determined I should qualify, so they sent me in the mornings to the best school available in Manchester, which dealt only in RAD ballet, the Imperial Society for Tap and musical comedy acrobatic. I immediately gained my Elementary with honours, so I continued teaching for the girls in the afternoons and Saturdays, proceeding with my exams in Manchester in the mornings. I also took ballroom.

My family was installed at Heald Green; our house was one of a series built around a tennis court with a clubhouse and a wide expanse of grass circling it. This was a joyful time, with weekends spent playing tennis with lots of friends. It was great to watch them playing in their whites, then later in the clubhouse playing table tennis, the gramophone playing. Sometimes as it grew dusk they played leapfrog around the court on the grass. There were about eight girls and boys, ages sixteen to nineteen, except for me, I was thirteen. I didn't play games but they accepted me and I loved to watch, so it didn't matter. They always ended up in our house for coffee. My sister met Rowland, her future husband. I also had an admirer, Ronnie Cliffe, a good tennis player and seventeen years old. He did remind me of Mickey Rooney. One day he said, "It's ridiculous you not playing, I'll teach you," so I found a pair of white shorts, and as arranged he appeared at my bedroom window at dawn. He had clambered up on the shed below. Of course I had forgotten about the arrangement and was asleep. I was and still am very absentminded about unimportant things.

The lesson was a disaster! Poor Ronnie! After retrieving and jumping the net dozens of times, he collapsed, realizing that games were not to be on one of my lists of achievements. To top it all an old gossip had seen us that early and complained my shorts were disgustingly too short. I didn't care, I loved just watching; actually that is something about my character: I'm never more happy than when others are enjoying themselves.

As teenagers we had a few halcyon, euphoric days. When not enjoying the tennis we often used to cycle through Moss Nook to Castle Mill. Rowland and I renovated an awful old bike for Maureen as a surprise. It was rusty black and extremely upright but we spent hours cleaning and painting it bright blue. Castle Mill was an outdoor swimming pool in idyllic surrounding. Other times we'd end up at Styal Woods. We discovered Gregg's Mill, which in those days was derelict and overgrown. Now it's National Trust with every facility, the Mill in working order, showing how the children and adults worked and were treated. Also they've renovated the cottages and shops to their original state.

We enjoyed our short freedom, Maureen riding rather regally on her upright bike, me struggling on Daddy's with the cross bar, and Rowland on a reasonably normal bike, but probably with his flies undone. He was good fun, intelligent, sensitive and apt to be absentminded, clumsy too. Mummy would say, "Move the china before he comes in." He and Maureen were already inseparable, still are in their eighties. Though were not a bit alike our voices were identical. She occasionally asked me to pretend I was her over the phone; this led to odd conversations with her many friends. Although Rowland said he knew, I don't think he did.

Who says teenagers are difficult, it's a bad time, a bad age? Rubbish! It was the happiest times of our lives. I was happy and fourteen, watching Maureen, Rowland and friends all enjoying themselves. We spent a memorable holiday with the Chappells, old Northenden friends of both my parents and grandparents. Frank Chappell had taught singing and piano to Mummy, Auntie Peggy and Maureen. The Chappells had a holiday house on Penhelig Terrace Aberdovey. We could look down onto the beach from the garden wall. When the tide was in we could step into the sea from the wooden steps. A rather important item in this story was the little ferry boat which ferried one across the estuary for a few pence. This small boat became of great importance later.

One night a party of us swam in the moonlight. The water was phosphorescent and softly outlined our bodies as we moved in the dark, silky water. Mrs Chappell, the perfect host, would have food waiting. She was an expert cook, preparing delicious bass caught by Peter Morris, Mary's brother. He was an avid angler. Mrs Chappell also baked her own bread and ham. I don't think many buffets today would match up to her table. Rowland was carrying a tray for her piled high with goodies, and his towel fell off. I remember no one assisting him while he stood helpless, unable to release the tray.

That time we enjoyed ourselves in Aberdovey seems unreal, a mirage, all young, uncaring, happy; but don't anyone dare reprimand us as we were so close to—in fact rubbing shoulders with—a living nightmare which would envelop us all too soon.

We had a party in Mrs Morris's upstairs room; her house was also on Penhelig Terrace overlooking the estuary. All were sixteen- or seventeen-year-olds except me. The names I can remember are Mary Morris, Rowland, Maureen, Robin and Philip. We made a great deal of noise. Robin pretended to play the piano with a few magnificent chords, then nothing. Mary married Philip. All the boys went to fight and I was later to meet Philip in Egypt during the war.

Perhaps it might be worth a mention that at this time, as the girls didn't pay me, I thought to make a little money. I polished the garage floor and gave a few private ballroom lessons, charging rather a lot. One boy aged about twenty-four (no boy) was most keen, but he became a nuisance. When I say this, there were no hands on, but he was not one of the gang and wanted to see me too often.

Anyway this period was a glorious time for all. Actually this was the time I lay on the lawn trying to retain the moment forever. Although I didn't know at the time, maybe it was a premonition, because that's when it happened: THE WAR STARTED!

Sadly all came to an end. The young men joined up; my Mickey Rooney shed his tennis whites for Air Force blue; Maureen's boyfriend Rowland became a navigator; the tennis court became a vegetable patch; and all the gardens had Anderson shelters. Daddy joined the A.R P., which met at the Heald Green Hotel. He couldn't have been much good with his dreadful sight and impaired hearing. Mummy and Maureen joined the M.T.C., driving all sorts of vehicles from Americans to articulated lorries. This was a strange few years. I was fourteen and the two girls were called up into the land army picking turnips. They didn't know what had hit them. I took over their school. Some of the proceeds paid for my continued studies, the rest went to them and the rent. I was extremely successful, actually enlarging the school, teaching RAD exams (not from a book). I also branched out, visiting schools and other towns.

Our family managed another holiday at Aberdovey, where the Outward Bound school used to take young men during the war who needed a rest before returning. I became friendly with one boy in particular, Claude—I used to call him Claudius. He was an officer in the Navy. I could never understand why he would never go in the water. One night on the beach I mithered as usual. As we sat on the sand he started to cry. It seems that he had spent hours on a raft holding his friends on; when eventually he was rescued he was alone and frozen.

Back at work I employed a pianist, Mrs Hall, a rosy-cheeked, correct little woman. Every Tuesday morning we set off for Holcombe Brooke Hall in Bury, a most grand abode owned by a lady with two children, Jill and Ann, aged fourteen and twelve. She employed me to take classes in her beautiful home, teaching her children, her many friends' children and her next-door neighbour Lady Hall's family as well. It was all quite ludicrous. I had to lie, saying I was eighteen. I hated the work. Imagine this beautiful room with its elegant grand piano and parquet floor, Mrs Hall sitting primly waiting for my orders, umpteen nannies, noisy children, and to top it all spaniel dogs getting in the way. Eventually I cracked; I just couldn't stand it. To Mrs Hall's horror I spoke, "That's it! Pack your music, Mrs Hall. We're going!" Poor Mrs Hall was so embarrassed. The strange thing was that Lady Hall and the others wrote to me offering to double my fee if I would return but I never did.

During the next three years I made extra money by taking private lessons, also a ballroom class above the Heald Green Hotel. Try and imagine this fifteen-year-old with a huge class of adults, most over forty because the war was on. I got the men to dance forward and around in an outer circle, with the ladies moving backwards in the inner circle while I would call out, "Slow, quick, quick, slow," to a gramophone playing Victor Sylvester records. It went down extremely well, possibly because drinks were brought up from the bar below.

I had one lucrative pupil, an elderly gentleman who wore black patent leather dancing shoes with large flat bows, had a slight balance problem and tilted backwards. I foolishly agreed to go with him, at a price, to the Ritz Ballroom Manchester, a favourite place for the forces to dance, particularly the Americans. We got into the middle of the floor, my partner lost his balance, fell on his back, and I fell on top of him. I just could not get up. To my horror a circle of Americans looked down on me. They eventually helped me when they had stopped laughing.

Through all this I seemed to retain a sort of naivety. According to others this caused me to drop terrible clangers; I believe this is still one of my faults, which is odd because I was much more adult than most of my age. To give you an example, two young men in the Fleet Air Arm took me home for tea. While they were in the kitchen discussing me, I listened at the hatch and heard, "Yes, she's certainly attractive, but isn't she dumb?" I was very upset and never stopped talking from that moment. It wasn't till years later that a man explained I had misunderstood their meaning.

My sister's twenty-first birthday arrived; she had a super party in the ballroom at the Heald Green Hotel. Grandpa supplied pounds of strawberries and asparagus from his garden at the Poplars. Strange, I can only remember my sister's birthday parties, but I cannot recall any of mine. I know for certain I had no twenty-first, but this was no one's fault as I was dancing at the time.

Before I go on, there's one place I feel should not be forgotten, The Roebuck, Mobberley, a lovely old inn offering exceptional food and a warm welcome. It was particularly popular with all the men flying at Ringway. They had a special tiny room upstairs with a small piano and such a low ceiling that even I could touch it. They so enjoyed themselves in that tiny room, where it was a rule that anyone who visited it signed the ceiling. Heaven knows whose names are on it, I'm not sure but quite possibly many famous names, Bader, Churchill, etc. All sorts when they came to Ringway came to the Roebuck. I know I signed it. Many, many years later I called and asked out of curiosity, "What's happened to the small room upstairs?" and the new owners exclaimed in horror, "Oh! That dirty room! We had it painted." I cannot swear to it but I feel that many wondrous names are hidden under that paint. I felt a sadness too for the many young men who had died and left their mark, but it was "that dirty room."

The war continued to rage. We often stood outside and listened to the enemy planes droning overhead and wondered who was next. It was rumoured that they used the river to guide them to Manchester. Mummy and Daddy felt that the Poplars was in danger as it backed on the river. They were right. On the first raid the bombers dropped an incendiary bomb on Grandpa's pear tree, the one that Donovan and I had built our tree house in. My grandparents put it out with buckets of water, but there was worse to come. The next morning Daddy went to work and said that the tram lines looked like a plate of spaghetti.

The following day the Poplars got what was called a direct hit by a land mine, which was a large bomb on a parachute. Granny heard it first give a glancing blow to the chimney. As Peter William was stone deaf, she set off to go and get him to the shelter, but as the bomb landed directly opposite, she got the full blast through the window and was badly hurt, her face covered in glass. The air raid wardens were on the scene quickly, and as the place was in complete darkness asked my grandmother to show them where everyone was, including the next-door neighbours. She helped them to find everyone, and it wasn't until then that she said, "I think I'm injured." The warden shone his torch on her face; they took her straight to hospital, where she stayed for weeks, her face eventually being hardly marked. The nurses said they spent hours removing glass. The warden said afterwards they were amazed at how calm she was and thought her very courageous.

Rowland and I managed to go into the Poplars the next

morning, although the police had cordoned it off as it was deemed unsafe and would have to be demolished. Not only did we need blankets but we hoped we might be able to save some of Granny's and Grandpa's treasures. They had still some beautiful things from their elegant past, but we could find nothing. The chest where she kept blankets had been opened, the blankets torn and covered with a soot; the glorious glass display cabinet with many beautiful articles in including a pair of brightly-coloured porcelain Punch and Judy decanters—I can visualize them now; they looked perfect but when I touched the cabinet they fell to dust! Blast is a strange thing. When we went to the stairs, there were none, just a stretched-out stair carpet like a slide. It was all very weird and eerie.

Anyway that was the end of the Poplars, no more luxury flat. My grandparents were again reduced to the poverty line, living almost in squalor in one room. Oddly they received no compensation for losing such a large and lucrative house. This was a mystery which was never solved. Everyone else did and some cheated and claimed more than they were entitled to. But they were alive, luckier than most. It had its amusing side too. Grandpa visited Gran in the hospital immediately. He had not bothered to wash, and like the blankets he also was covered in soot, and Grandma, seeing how upset he was, joked, "Good Heavens! Peter William, you look like a young man. Your hair and moustache are black!" She at that moment had a white cover over her face with holes cut for her eyes and mouth—very distressing.

From the age of fourteen I had numerous pianists whom I feel deserve a few words, as not only were they important but all had different and interesting personalities and all were kind and helpful. Top of the list of course was my mother; she always knew exactly what and how to play. Then came Mrs Dean, she of the husband with the beautiful voice whom I borrowed. She was a plump, neat, correct little woman, an old friend of the family. Once when playing in the school hall in Heald Green, she let out a cry, stopped playing and frantically delved down her bosom (which was ample and well-corseted), letting out short shrieks, not in the least Mrs Dean's normal behaviour. We all watched in amazement. Suddenly with a gasp of relief she pulled out a new potato and cried, "Thank goodness! It's only a potato. Mr. Robinson must have put it there!" Now I think that needs explaining: Mr Robinson was the greengrocer; Mrs Dean, being in a hurry, had leant forward holding her bag open, Mr. Robinson had tipped the potatoes in and one had escaped down her cleavage.

Mrs Moston was next on my pianist list. Mr and Mrs Moston and their two children Donovan and Marjory lived at Alder Briar next to the Poplars. She was a brilliant woman who wrote poetry under the name of Ben Moston. She was thought of highly by John Betjeman and wrote frequently for *Punch*, her poems being illustrated by Shepard. She also was honoured guest at Foyles London. She talked a great deal to me about music and life in general. I realize now her potential was never used, as she sacrificed it all for her husband. He was a good father and extremely handsome (Ben was not a pretty woman), but he was completely devoid of artistic temperament. He was not a romantic; in fact he was the complete opposite of his wife. I would say he did not understand why she wrote at all. It was a joy to take a class when she played with such feeling, and lovely classical music, but she only played when I was desperate and wouldn't accept payment.

The next was Mrs Hall, correct, prim, straightforward, and like a little red apple with her rosy cheeks. It was her job.

Last of all came Daddy, who only played once one Saturday. It wasn't easy as he couldn't play from music, and I had to know all the nicknames for the tunes that would be suitable for the exercises. There was the Shadow Dance, the Dum Di Dum tune and so on. It seems that he had actually been taught in Egypt by a famous musician called Busoni and had never forgotten his fingering, which was good.

My babies' classes always flourished even though I hated them. Every morning when I went for the bus to go for my studies I met a rather good-looking young man, who spoke to me one day. I as usual became rather nervous, stupidly saying, "Are you the father of one of my babies?" He looked horrified and I never saw him again. When I told my grandmother she exclaimed, "Will you never learn!" I still have the same problem of saying the wrong thing now.

We always had a special day for parents at the end of term, when all their little darlings would wear their party clothes and perform. They always started with the march, which was rather like the goose step. One three-year-old girl was particularly good at this, so she was to lead it. For some reason her father had come on his own. Off they started. She lifted her skirt up high and away she went with a magnificent goose step and no knickers!

When I read this it sounds to me like a telegram, there's so much between the lines unsaid, feelings and thoughts. I'm only writing a quarter of what was in my past; it's difficult, too, remembering, knowing it's exactly as it was. I certainly do not want to cheat, so am only putting into words that I'm most sure of; which times and places came first are not too important if incorrect, but the actual incidents must be right. There so many wonderful, interesting people I've encountered I just don't want to neglect them and turn them into forgotten souls.

At the time of Ronnie Cliffe (Mickey Rooney) I was also enthralled by a pilot called John Heaton, who was eventually billeted with us. He must have been about twenty-one. He would tease me about my short skirts, which annoyed me because I knitted them. The reason they were so short was because I used to get bored before they were long enough. He was immensely attractive, spoilt, and really (considering he wasn't in the least bit interested in a fourteen-year-old) was extremely patient with my continuous attention. In fact, our whole family must have been trying to a young heroic pilot, but he seemed to like us, particularly my father.

One night Maureen had the use of the car, so we set off to take John to the pictures in Gatley. Halfway there Maureen stalled the engine because she was new to driving. John jumped out, saying, "Hell! Let me drive, I'm terrified," which was quite funny when one realized he was actually fighting a war and would pass over our house making certain noises with his plane so we recognized him. Later I found out that he was always in trouble, although he never lost his commission.

I saw him twice at different times in my life, once in Egypt, the second time when the war was over. I was dancing in York with the Anglo-Polish Ballet over Christmas, and Mummy, Daddy and John spent Christmas with me. I remember being very unkind to him, saying, "I cannot think why I thought so much about you for so long, you're only a dirty old man." He must have been only about twenty-eight. Admittedly he had put on weight and looked older, but he laughed, saying I was cruel and unfair. Although he was a madcap he had fought and ended the war in what was called Popski's Army, which I believe was dangerous.

The war continued and we moved again, this time to an almost identical house to the Poplars, only about fifty yards farther on, also backing onto the river. This was Brookside and it was already turned into large substantial flats where we occupied the ground floor. I had one of the rooms as a studio and continued teaching. Some of the Royal Ballet while performing in Manchester rehearsed at the studio where I was studying. They became friendly and of course we had a party at Brookside. Many of the soloists came: Moira Shearer, Beryl Grey, Joan Sheldon and David Paltenghi. He was so good-looking, all the girls flattered him. I saw Moira and him dance together in *Les Pateneur*. It was breathtaking, both in sparkling white, she with her red hair and he so dark and handsome.

David seemed to take pity on me. Let's not be untruthful: I was seventeen, inclined to be overweight, and according to Moira, who gave me a lesson as a friend, I was extremely badly taught and already too old to dance ballet. But David offered to help me find digs if I ever went to London. This was going to happen sooner than I expected. I was entered for the Advanced RAD. This all sounds very grand, but exams were no entry then into the professional world, and it was all that Manchester could offer. Another candidate and I entered the exam room, dressed in our regulation outfit: white tutus, pink tights, and pink point shoes. Adeline Genee, a once-famous ballerina, and Felix Demery were the examiners. All went reasonably well until my partner was slipping badly and so nervous she couldn't spit in the rosin, an essential part of a dancer's life. She stood over the rosin box struggling to spit for what seemed ages while the examiners waited. Eventually I joined her and spat, not having any difficulty.

The next thing we were pirouetting singly across the room when I completely lost my sense of direction, ending sprawled across the examiner's table with my arms around Felix's neck. Later my teacher announced to the class, "Trust Meeta if there's a man." It made the class laugh but was quite untrue, and I should know. I sadly walked down the stairs, quite sure I had failed. When I met Adeline Genee she touched me gently on the cheek with her kid glove, saying, "Go to London now. Don't wait for your results, you'll do no good here!" This was most unusual, as the examiners never spoke to candidates. I felt honoured, and knew I must obey.

What about a spot of philosophy while I'm revving up for the next chapter. Sometimes I feel I'm not wholly one person; there's another intelligence lying dormant within my brain. Sometimes it wakes and I find myself thinking, *This isn't me*, but before I can recognize it it's gone! One thing's certain: it's far cleverer than I am.

2

My adventures begin. Memories are a bit like jigsaw pieces: so clear, yet I don't quite know where each piece goes. That's why I must write them down or they will disappear forever.

I was nearly eighteen. It was time to go so I arranged to meet David Paltinghi in London. I never lacked in approaching people or asking for anything, yet I had the most awful inferiority complex, a dreadful opinion of myself and my capabilities. This seems a strange mixture, as most people with my problem are intensely shy and shunned company. But not me, I was quite the opposite. I would go anywhere, ask any questions and had an insatiable curiosity about everything. Take for instance right at the beginning I asked a favour from the brilliant, sought-after

David. What an imposition! Women were literally falling around his feet. He too was well aware of this adoration, taking advantage quite outrageously, yet he didn't hesitate to help this plump, uneducated, talkative (don't forget I had overheard I was dumb), gullible Lancashire teenager. I certainly was the perfect country bumpkin, plunging head-on into the great city.

I took the midnight train from Manchester. Even this was exciting. I had a couchette and slept the night, arriving at Euston very early in the morning. The steward brought me a cup of tea, then I stayed until a reasonable hour before going to Lyon's Corner House, Leicester Square, for breakfast, a place I frequented every time I returned from home.

David met me and took me to the ten o'clock class in West Street, where Vera Volkova instructed most of the great dancers of that time. I stood at the barre performing my plie between Svetlana Beriosiva and Pamela May, both soloists with the Royal Ballet. I watched as their elegant legs wafted high above their heads while my too-sturdy legs stayed well below my shoulder. I struggled through and managed a few fouettes at the back, then stood in amazement as two by two they performed forty-four fouettes on point with a few doubles thrown in. But none were unkind. I was accepted and encouraged. I even pirouetted next to Balanchine, one of the great choreographers. But my audacity did not stop there. I asked the great teacher for a private lesson to assess my capabilities. Later some of the dancers told me that many of them wouldn't have dared to impose on Volkova, but she gave me my lesson that morning, spending more time than she needed. Her advice was, "You could be quite good, but not unless you train solidly for at least two years." Of course this was quite impossible as I could not afford it and had to find work soon. She understood and gave me the name of an agent who might help me.

David then took me to Mrs Hamilton's boarding house in

Notting Hill Gate, opposite the Mercury Theatre. She agreed to let me have a room cheaply, a tiny garret right at the top of the house. It only had a large skylight from which I could step out onto the roof. I don't think I would have got the room if it hadn't been for David. Then he took me to a rather swish restaurant where fish and lobster were swimming in a large tank and you chose your lunch live. This wasn't really my scene, but all out of this world for a seventeen-year-old. It was about three p.m. by this time and David left me.

I went straight to the agent and showed her all I could do. I tapped, did the splits and a little ballet, and her verdict was, "You're not very good, but with a lot of luck you might get taken for the Blue Bells. Here are a few auditions for the chorus, but these are not very classy shows."

I noticed on her desk a programme for the Anglo-Polish Ballet in Lewisham. It was a well-known ballet company that my grandmother had taken me to see at the Opera House Manchester. They always started their performance with a white classical ballet, either *Les Sylphide* or *Swan Lake*, and then finished their repertoire with the gay and colourful *Crakow Wedding* Polish dancing. I had never forgotten it. I asked the agent about them and she answered, "Yes, they've asked me for a dancer, but I'm sorry, dear, they're a ballet company way out of your league."

I tore up the addresses she had given me and set off for Lewisham. By the time I caught a bus it was dark and an air raid had begun. They always started about seven and lasted about an hour. I arrived at the stage door and gave the agent's name, saying she had sent me. The stage doorman seemed surprised, saying, "We didn't expect you till tomorrow. You can wait in the wings until the performance is over, and the director will see you after."

I stood in the wings and was transported into heaven! On the stage in the soft blue light was the ballet *Les Sylphide* poised still. As the curtain rose and the orchestra played Chopin's Nocturne the dancers began to float in their ethereal white frothy dresses with their tiny wings, the male dancer elegant in his black velvet and white satin.

Suddenly I was startled by a strange guttural voice: "Hello!" I looked and saw nothing. The voice came again: "Hello!" and my skirt was jerked sharply. I looked down and there was the smallest man I have ever seen, a dwarf. He explained he was the drummer and didn't play till the last ballet. I don't know why but I told him all about my deception. We shook hands and he wished me luck. Eventually it was the ballet *Crakow Wedding* with Alicia Halama the bride and Konarski the groom. It was a riot of colour and Polish celebration, then it was all over.

The stage was in darkness, the scenery had been rolled up and all was quiet, with just a bare, stark bulb shining down. I felt nervous, my mouth dry. What was I going to do? A tall blonde man came toward me, held out his hand and said in a soft American accent, "Jasph Crandall, hi!" I couldn't believe it! He was a soloist from the Diaghlief Ballet. I could hardly breathe. The soft voice continued, "Do you like auditions, honey?" I managed to answer, "No." I held on to the wooden case nearby, my legs very weak. I heard him say, "No, neither do I, I'm exceptionally tired. Okay, honey, start on Monday at Hull, ten o'clock sharp." He kissed my hand and was gone.

I was a member of a ballet company, a good one, and hadn't done a step! To give you the magnitude of this achievement, think of someone not good enough to pass one A level and getting a place at Cambridge! But what was going to happen next?

I sat in my small garret thinking of all that had happened to me in one day, when there was a tap at the window. A young man was crouching down on the roof. He introduced himself as Peter Wright, a dancer with the Royal Ballet, and asked if I fancied some stew. Quite honestly by this time I was ravenous. I later learnt that his stews were well-known, whether because they were awful or what I don't know, but I enjoyed it. We ate happily and I did notice that there seemed to be every ingredient in it, including raisins.

Next morning I got to know Mrs Hamilton, who invited me for tea in her kitchen. She struck me as an extremely hard-bitten landlady, but she seemed to have a soft spot for me. She had a slight European accent and wore at all times a rather odd outfit: a cotton print overall buttoned down the front with nothing underneath, not even pants. A good thing she wasn't going to perform the goose step! She agreed to keep my room at half price even if I wasn't there.

I gradually got promoted to much better accommodation with a shared kitchen. This room, although nice, had a dividing door which my bed head was against. The actress who had the adjoining room had her bed head flush against mine. As she was frequently visited by a well-known person from the Opera Covent Garden, this proximity became very embarrassing, as I felt I was in bed with them. I did move the bed but it didn't improve much.

Talking of incidents in bedrooms, I once allowed a girl and her friend, a one-legged Air Force boy, to stay. Their excuse was they had missed the last train and he couldn't walk far, so they piled into my bed—I couldn't really see why not—but I finished up on the floor, realising that friends or no, an amorous one-legged man was too much for me.

I rang my parents explaining all and then continued on to Hull to book as cheap a room as possible. My goodness, it was cheap, too! My first impression of this next landlady was a buxom, frowsy but jolly fifty-year-old woman. What impressed me the most were her large feet encased in shoes that were not sandals, but the sole had burst from the upper part, displaying a row of fat toes. I liked her and we agreed on a rent of only a few shillings for bed (including fleas) and supper. I was as pleased as punch.

The room was terrible, big and bare with two wooden chairs, a wooden table, two beds and no carpet. Daddy came to see what I was up to and although he didn't pass any judgement, he quietly offered to install me in a hotel. I was just so thrilled with my achievements so far, I wouldn't hear of it and invited him to stay the night. My landlady was overjoyed and did offer me an alternative room so my father could be on his own, but when I found that I would have to share with some sailors, I declined. That evening our host entered our room triumphantly with fish and chips in the paper, a fork each and a mug of tea. Daddy returned home probably in a daze. Hull was getting bombed rather heavily but shows went on. We didn't bother much.

No one seemed to notice me at the theatre. I enrolled, then kept in the background and did class well hidden behind the scenery. I found out that all new girls danced witches in the ballet *Faust*. I enquired about a rehearsal and was told, "That's not necessary, you just put rags on from the skip basket at the side of the stage and follow the other witches. It's easy. They just crawl on the stage, clawing and recoiling and sometimes jumping."

This all sounded very easy. The stage was dark with lighting resembling flames. Faust (Konarski) was crouching in centre stage. The witches would gradually surround and engulf him in the dark; he would disappear and the devil (Pavinoff) would appear in his place. The witches crawled off and the drum would roll (my gnome doing his bit). This was Pavinoff's piece de resistance. He would amaze the audience by commencing his solo with his unbelievable pirouette. He was famous for this feat and had been known to do a phenomenal twenty on one leg (five was brilliant). I was crawling and jumping quite happily with the rest of them when they started to crawl rapidly backwards. My rags fell over my eyes, I slightly lost my bearings, and there was a deadly hush. There didn't seem to be anyone about.

I lay with my cheek on the soft, warm boards when suddenly

a large white spot came on me. I looked right. There was a foot encased in sparkling white kid. I looked left. There was another similar foot poised. I turned slowly, looking upwards. There, directly above, was an immaculate crotch. I had crawled directly between the devil's feet, so he could not possibly do his pirouette! Realising where I was, I crawled at full speed into the wings, joining the other horrified witches. There was a most unholy row, Pavinoff swearing that it had been done on purpose by the company to ruin his entrance, and he left the company. No one ever mentioned me. Nothing more was said.

The next week was in Chatham. I got much better digs with quite a decent family and they had an Anderson shelter in the garden and a Morrison shelter in the kitchen. The idea of a Morrison was that it served as a table too. This family had a routine. When there was an air raid Dad would stand outside the open door and shout instructions. If it got really bad we all trooped down to the Anderson shelter. This night things went quicker than expected. Dad suddenly shouted, "Dive!" so we all dived under the Morrison table, Mum, two girls (about eleven), the dog, me, and lastly Dad. Except for the loud explosion that followed it was funny because there wasn't really room, and bottoms were left exposed.

Actually the bombs weren't as bad as the rats! The theatre was overrun and every morning we found large sticky traps set. I think the reason was that a lot of old buildings were being demolished, which probably disturbed them. There was even an amusing side to this. These rats used to eat our ballet shoes and Vera's knickers. Poor Vera! She always had a rather superior air about her, and being the only one whose knickers the rats ate caused a great joke.

On the notice board it announced all the corps de ballet on stage, rehearsal for *Les Sylphide*. Maria Sanina, alias Bridget Kelly, was taking rehearsal. She abruptly called, "Where's the new girl? Come in with the first three." She called to the pianist, "The finale please." The pianist started to play Chopin's lively mazurka. The two dancers started off across the stage, and I struggled with a travesty of their steps, ending up with a sort of gallop to keep up. Bridget scathingly screamed, "Stop! What on earth do you think you are doing? Leave the stage this instant!" I slunk away down the stone steps, knowing the sack was inevitable.

Passing the office on my way down, the committee, which consisted of three Poles, stopped me. They were Jan Cobel, the extremely wealthy owner, a horrible little man, oversexed with a big strong body and very short legs; Demidetzki, the manager, a tall, nice man about thirty; and Konarski, brilliant dancer, very attractive, but afraid of his wife Halama, who was glamorous and brilliant too. They all wore black overcoats and black homburgs and they reminded me of three black crows. When they saw me they beckoned. They spoke little English but pushed a contract under my nose, which I signed at once. I never liked signing anything, but I felt this must be better than the sack. They seemed delighted, not knowing of course that I was redundant.

On reading the contract I found that I had agreed to be loaned to the Jack Hilton Merry Widow Show, at that time playing successfully in the West End. Five other girls and I were to take the place of the French cancan dancers, who incidentally had been bringing the house down. It seems that the War Office felt that the forces deserved better entertainment. It had suddenly been decided that two London shows of high quality should be sent abroad post haste. The Ballet was too large a company so it was agreed for some of their dancers to be sent with another company and stay out to rejoin the Ballet on their arrival. The Merry Widow company thought that six English girls would behave in a more seemly manner than the six French ones; I wouldn't like to argue on that point. Anyway everyone was happy, especially me. There turned out to be only three girls loaned from the Ballet; the other three came from the London club the Pigalle.

The next thing I found myself with the other two dancers being wined and dined at an extremely expensive hotel by Jan Cobel. We drank champagne and vowed to uphold the good name of the Ballet while dancing elsewhere. Jan Cobel stood and read haltingly in English a small pep talk of farewell.

We spent a lot of time at Drury Lane, Covent Garden, where all the stars congregated before going abroad, signing papers, getting our passports, etc., then we had to have all our inoculations, one of which caused us all to faint in the oddest places: Vera in a restaurant, slipping quietly under the table; Marianne Balchin (daughter of the novelist) on the escalator; and I travelling home for the last time. The train was packed with soldiers with Christmas leave. We had to stand in the corridors, and the next thing I heard a voice in the distance, "Please, miss, I'll have to move you, you're sitting on my Christmas pudding." The young soldier heaved me up, settling me elsewhere. We both were going home for a few days before leaving England.

But I'm jumping the gun. Three weeks earlier we had gone through some very strange rehearsals. Like everything I came in contact with, things never seemed to progress in a normal manner. The man allotted to arrange and take rehearsals was John Pygram, an excellent dancer, quiet, unassuming, shy, and completely unable to put two steps together, never mind creating a breathtaking cancan. We did absolutely nothing for three weeks. I received the normal half pay rehearsal money. I felt very wealthy living in my small garret with money to spare.

Then came the last rehearsal before the show. Everyone was present on stage: Madge Elliot, Cyril Richard, also a young handsome man called Terrance Alexandra, who later was the millionaire in the television series *Bergerac*. When our music commenced we did nothing! How could we? We'd learnt nothing! Cyril Richard was obviously extremely annoyed and distressed, but with great dignity he approached, saying, "This is not your fault. We have no time as the show starts tomorrow, so you and I together must create a cancan, ballroom scene, and the rest tonight!"

So with his fantastic experience and showmanship and our strange mixture of different abilities, three nightclub girls, two classical ballet dancers and one expert in creating dances for babies such as giants, fairies, trees and mushrooms prepared for the show! What on earth could we do to compare with the show-stopping cancan dancers from Paris? Well, I like to believe that our efforts were by no means a disgrace. The applause we got was more than generous.

Cyril asked us in turn what we were best at, as in a cancan one is supposed to surprise and excite the audience with her daring and amazing feats! Marianne Balchin could, thank goodness, do excellent overs and cartwheels while we all waved our skirts and showed our knickers. Sadie and I pirouetted across and around the stage, and Pamela managed to hop centre stage while holding her leg to her ear, just like the cancan dancer in Lautrec's painting. We all managed to jump into the splits while letting out a loud scream! Cyril Richard thanked us for our efforts, then quietly told us to say no more about John's failure. He was to dance the Gold and Silver Waltz in the Maxim's scene with Diana Gould, which she had arranged. We all liked John even though he seemed to be devoid of personality, so we were glad he wasn't penalized.

Our costumes were gorgeous, the cancan dresses crimson bombazine laced tightly and underlined with mountains of white frills, black suspenders, black stockings and shoes, and white frilly knickers which (this is important) were gathered on a tape, enabling them to be ironed more easily. For the ballroom scene we all wore different ballgowns and fans. My dress was many layers of blue and grey chiffon, but a little too long. Vera's I could never forget. It was extremely tight down to her ankles, in bright yellow taffeta with bands of black velvet. She was so slim, just like a stick of rock. I complained to Mrs Bliss, the wardrobe mistress, that mine was too long, but she did nothing. The first night of the show as we came down the sweeping staircase in the ballroom scene, Cyril Richard, resplendent in evening dress, met us one by one and did a few steps with us. When it came to my turn I waltzed backwards up my skirt; Cyril Richard was unable to keep hold of me so I fell flat on my back in the middle of the stage with the star gazing down at me. Cyril with his usual kindness forgave all. My dress was immediately shortened.

Sometimes it's so easy to write this all down just as it happened; it all seems as fresh as if it was yesterday. Then suddenly, horrors of horrors! a void appears, my mind is blank, the names of the ship, the place, the time…gone. I have only one excuse, and beg the reader's forgiveness: it is quite a few years ago. In the short span I spent on the stage I went on seven ships, one aeroplane and two very odd train journeys, and I did not take notes or keep a diary. Oh well! Back to my story.

The rehearsal and first show were behind us, it was Christmas Eve, and we were in the foyer of a theatre somewhere near London. I remember…Oxford! It was dark, the only light coming from the lit signs of the exits, ladies and gents. We'd been issued with one blanket and a camp bed each. As it was extremely cold I suggested to Pamela we put our beds together, put one blanket underneath and one on top of us. That night Pamela told me about herself and Sadie, the other girl we knew very little about. She was older than us, intelligent and spoke fluent Italian; in fact she was a bit of a loner and a mystery. Sadie and Pam had both been showgirls at the famous Pigalle Club in the West End. They didn't dance, just paraded on the catwalk with enormous fantastical headdresses on and little else, so of course they were incredibly beautiful, Sadie a natural blonde with mauvy blue eyes, Pamela dark and willowy with soft, velvety brown eyes and lashes so long and luxurious people were always asking were they false.

I realise now Pamela was shallow and spoilt with no morals whatsoever and a quick temper, quite unlike my mother, who was just as beautiful, just as spoilt, but clever with quite a different temperament.

The next morning we embarked with hundreds of troops onto a magnificent liner. One had an odd feeling as one walked up the gangplank of this beautiful ship, which once had been the conveyer of people on journeys of happiness. Many embarking now would never return and probably were full of apprehension and fear. This did not apply to me, as I was not going to fight and had no fear.

I shared a pleasant cabin with Marianne and Vera. We had a luxury bathroom but there was only one drawback: when we had a bath or shower it was saltwater. They supplied us with special soap, which was quite useless. The voyage went smoothly except for one slight hitch. It was announced that we had engine trouble and we had to slow down while repairing it, so we could not keep up with the convoy, which meant we became rather vulnerable all alone. We were told, therefore, not to undress for bed and to keep our life jackets ready. Very reassuring! We felt very sad as we waved the convoy goodbye. That night the ship dropped depth charges (that's a strange feeling; the whole ship shudders). The rumour was that there was an enemy submarine lurking nearby. Luckily the repairs did not take too long and we were able to join another convoy the next day.

We arrived in Alexandria, my father's birthplace, very late and were put in the most disgusting hotel: very sleazy, lots of red, low lights and horrible room facilities; I can see the dirty cracked washbowl now. We put furniture against the door and listened to our door handle being turned and other noises all night. The next morning we were transferred immediately to an exemplary hotel. Vera and I never found out what had gone wrong, but we knew we had been put in a brothel, it was said by mistake. Many strange things happened in Egypt! We now were in a magnificent hotel. I had a pot of coffee and goat's milk brought to our room every morning and sat on the veranda watching the busy street below. The Egyptians loved to make noise, particularly the taxis, which hooted and tooted all the time, not in a cross way but with big smiling faces. There was a never-to-be-forgotten cacophony of noise unlike anywhere else.

All during our tour I never stopped practicing on my own, getting Marianne and Vera to teach me all the steps in the Anglo-Polish Ballet's repertoire so no time was wasted. I became friendly with two New Zealand sergeants who were helping out as extras in the ballroom scene and Maxim's Club. They had been in the Middle East a long time and showed me around. I cannot remember all but we saw some splendid gardens and had some wonderful meals the three of us. I often shared the cost, although most girls chose officers who seemed to have plenty of money. Lloyd did attempt to become more than a friend, but I think he became resigned…well, almost. He was a really nice boy and he came to the rescue one day when I really needed him.

The show went on successfully. Our next destination was Cairo, where we were to spend quite a long time. Our hotel was truly excellent. Vera and I shared a beautiful room with another large balcony. We were to perform at the Cairo Opera House (I wasn't doing badly for someone who wasn't good enough for a second-rate show). What a theatre! Our ballroom scene had everything: sweeping staircase down centre, magnificent chandeliers, rotating stage for Maxim's Club—all most exciting. King Farouk came to watch, sitting in the royal box on his own. I was worried because he had the most terrible reputation. An English girl had disappeared. I said I wasn't going to risk him taking a fancy so would keep my face covered with my skirt. The others laughed, saying, "I don't think he's interested in your face."

The royal box was right next to the stage on our left. Farouk had been so handsome; now, still very young, he was fat and so ugly, with a big black beard that was said to cover diseased skin. Queen Farida and her daughters came the following night. They were exceedingly beautiful. It seems that Farouk had discarded her because she had only daughters.

I don't know where to start; so many extraordinary things happened in Cairo. I really loved Cairo for all its strange habits. I suppose the first incident was when John Heaton phoned. Vera took the message as I was out. She said it sounded most odd. I had to get a tram late that night to where a man would meet me. This I did and was taken into the desert, where I was told to be quiet and walk a few yards ahead where I would meet John, but we must talk in whispers, also I must leave immediately they called me. John was waiting there. We chatted in whispers. I tried to tell him bits of news from home. It seems he was under guard, having misbehaved, but a friend had arranged for our meeting. We had about ten minutes, then I was whisked away in a great hurry. He wrote to me explaining that they had transferred him from the Air Force. He became a captain in Popski's Army, which I heard was a rather dangerous unit.

The company became friendly with the 8th Army, who invited us for lunch in their camp in the desert. I got taken for a ride in a Churchill tank, which was just like sitting in a tin can, a very big tin can. I seemed to sit in the middle with my feet dangling and there seemed to be a man above me. There was a square hole in front but all I could see was lots of sand as we climbed, then there was a clunk and all I could see was sky. We seemed to be travelling quite fast, with this constant clonking sand then clunking sky, not really a scenic tour, but an unforgettable experience just the same. After this I staggered covered in sand into the large tent to meet the army officers. I was handed (I was desperate for a drink) a whiskey sour. Now honestly! Why? It's whiskey with gritty sugar stuck around the rim. Someone said it was probably so you didn't notice the sand, which got into everything.

All the Merry Widow Company were invited to an extremely rich Syrian's twenty-first party (l hope I've got that right; I'm sure they said they were Syrians, not Egyptians.) The boys from the 8th Army were most concerned, not wanting the girls to go, but Cyril Richard insisted, saying it would be rude to refuse. I remember these young army officers giving us such a talk before we went, and seeming really worried.

The place the party was held was palatial, the buffet like something I've never seen before. But I was not in a party mood. I went around trying to find one of our dancers who wanted to go home early, but with no luck, as everyone was having a great time. At last a French journalist I had met before said he had to work early and was glad to escort me to my hotel. One of the young Syrians took us to the garage and left us, and we found we were locked in with absolutely no way out. There were many cars. My goodness, what cars! You could turn them into beds. There were bars inside with every drink imaginable. My Frenchman said, "Well, there's nothing we can do till someone leaves the party, so let us find the most comfortable car and wait." Luckily I found an umbrella, so the Frenchman got whacked frequently until I think he fell asleep from exhaustion. It was a long night; the party went on till dawn. When we got to the hotel the Frenchman (I can't remember his name) had breakfast with me. I'll give him the benefit of the doubt. Maybe he didn't know we were going to get locked in, and you cannot blame him for trying.

Ronnie Cliffe said he tried to see me but it seems he always arrived at the place two days after I had left. The husband of Mary Morris, sister of Peter, who used to catch the lovely bass for Mrs Chappell to cook at Aberdovey, was in the army. I managed to meet him in Cairo. He was so pleased and took me for lunch. We reminisced about Penhelig Terrace and our moonlight swims from the wall. He took me as a special treat to have my fortune told at the Blue Mosque, where an old Arab made marks in the sand. He foretold I would have four children—two boys would be born with red hair and would survive, the other two would not—I would touch the shores of Egypt once more, and I would be married twice. He got it all correct except I never married again.

For some reason, just before we left the theatre in London, my mother went all motherly and asked Mrs Bliss, the wardrobe mistress, if she would chaperone me. I wasn't particularly keen on this woman, whose husband Mr Bliss, a small portly man, was the conductor. She felt herself rather important and I never had anything to do with her until one day at about eleven o'clock when she approached me, saying, "I wish you to meet a gentleman now."

I was not in the least bit interested, but she was adamant I must do as I was told. The next minute I found myself in a quiet corner of the hotel alone with a Turkish officer about thirty years old. He offered me a drink, and thinking quickly I decided on fruit juice. He clicked his fingers at the waiter and our drinks arrived. I had only taken a few sips before I realised something was wrong. I jumped up and ran to the stairs, already feeling very strange, things growing and receding at a rate of knots. I saw in a blur about six of the Syrians whose party I had been to. I joined them, feeling there was safety in numbers. I then found myself at the head of the centre table in this opulent dining room having lunch, believing I had had a lucky escape. Surely lunch would put me right. Vera said later she had seen me and wondered at my odd behaviour. I didn't seem to improve, so managed to escape to my room. Looking in the mirror, which seemed to zoom backwards and forwards, my eyes were all black pupils. Suddenly, to my horror, I felt arms around me, strong arms! One of the young

Syrians had followed me. He wore a dark suit, so through my blurred vision I could see his flies were already undone. He pushed me against the table, and while I grappled with him the phone rang. This is the odd part: I answered it; Lloyd was waiting to take me swimming. Instead of screaming for help I calmly said (this was difficult because my speech was affected and my mouth was restricted; it seemed to be full of plums), "Tell him I'll be down in a minute." Amazingly I got rid of this slobbering, awful man with scathing remarks on his appearance, especially the bare parts. I've never been so nasty. It wasn't like me at all, but it worked and he went.

Lloyd was marvellous. He soon realised what had happened and he immersed me continuously in water, gave me copious doses of coffee, and put up with my ludicrous behaviour, cries such as "I'm safe, I'm safe! I love you, Lloyd. You're my bestesttish friend." This all added to innumerable cuddles. Poor Lloyd, this must have been a young man's nightmare. So much for my mother's chaperone!

Vera and I did the usual tourist things. We rode our camels and saw the Sphinx and pyramids. A photograph arrived of us both on our camels, addressed not to Meeta Thomas but "Metatatamus," which I thought amusing.

I have lots of photographs of our adventures, one particular one of the ballroom scene with Vera looking like a stick of rock, Pamela trying to look dignified, the two New Zealanders in evening dress and Cyril Richard, suave and elegant, poised under the chandelier ready to dance with us.

As always I seemed to get into trouble on stage and off, but Cyril Richard was more than generous to me and he called me his Lancashire girl, not, I believe, because of an accent (Daddy had seen that we spoke well), but because of my terrible clangers and the odd scrapes I got into. I think the worst on stage was once, just as I was entering onto the revolving stage in Maxim's Club, Lloyd said "There's a tape hanging down!" I said, "Pull it quickly," which he did. I could do nothing as I was holding my voluminous skirt high. It was the drawstring; my knickers fell to my ankles and I wondered why I could not lift my legs, but soon realised and made a most undignified hobble off stage.

Centre Cyril Richard, on his right me, on his left Vera

Another occasion Vera had a mishap. The Muslims would go down on their knees and pray at the oddest times. Vera had a terrible cold so she left her hanky in the wings on a box. At a convenient moment she darted off into the dark wings, picked up what she thought was her handkerchief, blew her nose, and then realised she had lifted the white cap of a praying Muslim. I asked her, "What did you do?" She replied, "I put it back."

How can one explain or describe the effect Egypt had on a nineteen-year-old girl who never thought she would ever travel farther than Northenden? Bananas were the first thing that impressed me, as we didn't have any in England, because of the war I suppose. I ate so many I couldn't bend down in my too-tight cancan dress, so Pamela couldn't do her high kicks over my head. I had to reduce my intake of the said fruit.

Then there was the market, an experience of exotic aromas, sounds and colours, nothing like the markets I was used to. As you walked in you were enclosed by what seemed like half-tents, half-buildings, open-fronted, selling all sorts of exciting objects. As I passed by, a young man in a tarboosh beckoned, inviting me in. I told him, "I can't buy anything, I've no money left." He replied that it did not matter, saying, "Come and have a coffee." I walked into what seemed like a set for the Arabian Nights. There was more than one room; all were lavishly carpeted and opulently furnished, the low ceiling consisting of beautifully draped material. I sat at a circular shiny brass table and was offered their wonderfully strong coffee. He asked me to stand before a tall, ornate mirror while he swiftly and expertly wound yards of heavy white satin around me. I was transformed into a bride with bows and train. I gazed in the mirror, saying, "I'm not thinking of getting married." I cannot remember his remarks, but he seemed quite happy just to dress me up in his fabulous fabrics.

I was sorry to leave Egypt, but we embarked on a ship for Italy on another luxurious liner with a great many Americans on board. I soon became friends with a large group. The ship was dry but my friends introduced me to rum and Coke. One morning on deck they suddenly said, "Sit down; don't move, whatever you do." I sat feeling rather foolish as the captain came up and had a conversation with me. There I was in the middle of the deck with my long circular skirt spread out. The reason for this, I found out when the captain had left, was that there were umpteen bottles of rum under my skirt! Being constantly curious, I went to see where my four American paratroopers slept. I thought it was awfully claustrophobic, lots of hammocks very close together down below the decks. They told me they were convicts allowed out on condition they joined this special unit. I really don't know if they were teasing me, but I didn't feel they were.

I don't know whether this is worth repeating, but for someone who had started out feeling a complete failure, I sometimes thought I was dreaming.

As the ship was full of Americans they had a special boxing match arranged in the centre of the deck. I was invited to sit with them right at the front, up above the ring. They explained that some of the men did not like boxing but it gave them certain privileges.

We arrived in Naples. This time I stayed with Pamela and once again our hotel was very nice, our room having a balcony overlooking the Bay of Naples. Nowadays people would pay a lot to have such a view. There was one odd thing: we had camp beds. We hadn't got a full orchestra so made it up with Italians. When the bombing got noisy our Italian musicians disappeared, which made our music rather weedy. The lights would go out, then the forces would shine their torches onto the stage.

All the time I was away I never really felt threatened or afraid of any man. I always put my trust in them. There were just a few occasions when things got out of hand, but then it was always the men who came to the rescue.

One time we were asked to go into a place where they were dancing, just hundreds of soldiers, none above the rank of sergeant. We always felt that the officers were privileged and certainly never saw any English girls, so whenever we got the chance we tried to mix. But this time it got a little out of hand. The men queued and danced in turn with us. Vera and I were whizzed around by black, white, big and small, faster and faster until I suddenly became afraid as they started to get aggressive and were pulling me from both sides. One man must have realised we were in danger of being pulled in half and called the MPs, so we were rescued. We did the same thing once on board ship. The soldiers on the lower deck sent us a message that we were too snooty to go and dance with them, so much to the officers' concern we went. It got a bit rough then, but not quite so bad. We survived talking and dancing with as many boys as possible. When we were at exhaustion point some men stepped in and rescued us, but that time I did not feel afraid.

One night the bombing had been rather severe, and after the show I had gone for supper up in the hills. On returning I was dropped off at my hotel, the officer carrying on downhill to his barracks. The building next to us had been damaged; I learnt later that a WAC had unfortunately been killed. There was no one in the hotel. I went to bed, but the next morning there was no breakfast, nobody about, no staff, no nothing. I went down into the kitchen, got myself something to eat, then started down the road, where I met the rest of the company. It seems that there was an unexploded bomb outside our hotel, so everyone had been evacuated.

In the shops they sold large salami sausage, which my father loved. He used to come home with delicious bread, salami and olives from a delicatessen called Brumes in Manchester. I couldn't resist buying some for him and hung it in the wardrobe, a fatal mistake! That night I woke to see Pamela's hand hanging over the side of the bed, her beautiful red nails being chewed by an enormous rat! We both screamed until the staff came. I don't know how they got rid of them, but I have never seen such huge animals, as big as cats, climbing up the balcony window clawing frantically to get in. I suppose as in Hull and Chatham the bombing had disturbed their habitat.

Another group of Americans, about six of them, invited me to a villa they shared in a lovely spot up in the hills. We all sat with our feet up on a rail around a stove, only my feet wouldn't reach. We were to have roast turkey, which one of them cooked, then walked around us carrying the turkey on a large plate, singing opera in a wonderful baritone. (Isn't it strange how certain moments stick in one's mind, some sad, some full of warmth and enjoyment?)

One night I was long gone to bed when my paratroopers disgraced themselves; they got very drunk and got into the singers' bedroom. The singers were older than us and rather fuddy-duddy. My friends, I learnt, had behaved in a rather ungentlemanly manner, attempting to kiss these matronly ladies. As Pamela remarked, "They should be so lucky!"

When I heard about the whole thing, I couldn't see they had been so awful, only having a bit of fun. They soon left the singers alone. Once again Pamela remarked, "That's probably why they complained." Some of them did look like Dick Emery's rendering of the spinster, who used to say, "I do like you."

My paratroopers yelled "Geronimo!" when they left the ladies, and loudly jumped down some wooden steps, wrecking them completely! When I saw the damage I couldn't believe my friends had done it. They were supposed to be punished by the army, but it all seemed to be forgotten.

I went the next night to their wonderful club. The Americans had taken over a place like a palace. The ornate ceilings stand out in my mind; the ceiling of the bar was heavily carved wood painted gold, red, blue and green—most unusual, but of course the Italians were unable to do anything inartistic. They did have a reputation of not being very brave, but I felt that their genius for creating beauty made up doublefold for any faults they may have been thought to have had. I saw General Patton at the American club. He stood out as he was taller than anyone else.

Another time Pam and I were invited to a party on a ship. For some reason we missed the boat that took us to it, so we got a lift from a local fisherman whose boat happened to be full of herrings. I slipped of course and fell headlong into them. I was not only wet through but smelt awful!

On arrival on board the young officers took me to the captain's cabin, where I showered and put on the sailors' clothes given me. I often wondered why nothing I did seemed to go smoothly but it never stopped me enjoying myself. As usual I did a tour of the ship, always nosey. In fact I explored battleships, liners, aircraft carriers, even the planes coming up on a sort of lift. I did try a submarine but thank goodness it didn't submerge; I don't like water over my head.

How those men coped I cannot imagine. They always, whatever their job, gave the appearance of being happy and were friendly and caring. This applied to English, Americans, Poles, French and Belgians, except when they became unhinged, and some of these I did encounter. One was an officer in the army I didn't actually know. His behaviour was noticeably difficult and aggressive. What was strange was that the other men obviously guarded him.

On one occasion Vera, some of the other girls and I were giving the men an impromptu performance of part of *Sylphide* when this man suddenly flipped and was going to strike me. His friends intervened and the episode was smoothed over. But then a more serious thing happened. I was swimming at a club when someone got hold of me and dragged me under. I was very frightened, and for what seemed ages struggled for my life. It was the same man. Eventually his friends managed to rescue me. When I had recovered, they pleaded with me to say nothing. They said they cared for him and would soon have him on a ship home, so I forgot the episode. Some men became so irrational coming home I know they were locked up.

Now, sadly, my memory cannot remember exactly where I was, but what I can recall was once being disguised in an army coat and cap, being smuggled in somewhere, and finding myself fifty yards from the front line. When the guns fired the enemy line was all lit up. I could see the men running about opposite me; they looked about an inch tall.

During my stay in Naples I befriended an army man who had something to do with the opera in Naples, so I went often, sometimes taking some of the other girls. We sat in the royal box, to the annoyance of the principals of our show, who had a much inferior box. This army officer suggested I stayed on and helped with the dancing in the opera but I refused, as all I wanted was to dance, improve, and be able to return and be accepted by the Anglo-Polish Ballet.

Maybe this story seems to consist of a stream of parties, but we were there to entertain the troops. How my associates carried out their duties I have no idea; I just did my best going out and talking to as many soldiers as I could, more often than not in a group. I also tried not to always mix with officers only, as I knew quite well from listening to the other ranks how they felt left out.

One night we all went to an RAF camp, which seemed to be

in a large Nissan hut. Typically there didn't seem to be any food laid on, so I found myself wielding a large frying pan, cooking huge amounts of eggs and bacon for everyone. That night one young airman arranged to take me out one night. He never came; instead another boy came in his place. They never said why, but I understood that when this happened a young man usually had not returned from a mission.

Being young we used to laugh and joke when one of our RAF friends would jerk oddly, throwing whatever he was holding up in the air, especially awkward if it was a drink. He had a form of shellshock. It seemed he preferred us to laugh about it. Hopefully after a rest he recovered.

Our visit to Pompeii was unforgettable. The whole company went. Of course there were no tourist crowds so I was able to walk all on my own down the streets so heavily laden with past memories. I don't care how people scoff; no one could help but feel the atmosphere, which of course was far stronger with no other people around.

I suddenly came to a queue of soldiers waiting to go into a building at the end of the street, so I asked if I could join them. They had a short discussion, then huddled round me, saying, "If you put this army coat and hat on and keep very quiet we'll take you with us." In we went. To my surprise the first thing as we entered was a large penis on a weighing machine! Then followed lots of little square rooms, each with large paintings on the back wall. I couldn't contain my curiosity any longer, asking, "Are they acrobats?" In between the laughter the soldiers said, "For goodness sakes! Be quiet or we shall all be in trouble." When we came out they bought me a little book, which was kind because they were only in the ranks; I've got that book to this day. When I joined the rest of the company it seemed that ladies were quite forbidden to go where I had been.

After that escapade we all had yummy spaghetti with tomato.

The guide insisted on showing me how to eat it correctly. To the amusement of everyone he fed me so quickly I was covered in it. But for all that, it's a day I'll never forget. We were sitting outside the restaurant with the volcano, Cyprus trees and Pompeian statues in sight. I bought a watercolour of the scene from an artist sitting there for a few lire.

Here again my memory fails me. I can't remember whether it was Vesuvius or Etna, but one of them was rumbling and erupting flames all the time. One day I went shopping in a white dress when suddenly it started raining—but it was raining mud. I was covered. Much later the volcano did erupt and destroyed a village nearby. We went to see the quite extraordinary sight. The village was buried under light grey ash. It was rumoured that the reason for the eruption was because an American had fallen into the volcano!

We all went to a party one night after the show where there was a marvellous pianist with a face like a frog, performing and singing jazz! To my disgust, as always, no food (I was always hungry after the show) and no drink. The place was full of high-ranking Americans all talking. I, fed up, went and found a young sergeant in charge of stores, so together we went looking for and found some sandwiches. Looking in the medical stores I saw about a gallon of pure alcohol; I hate to own up to such stupidity (but this book, however painful, is the truth and nothing but). We also found large tins of grapefruit juice.

I went behind the bar, doling out sandwiches and drinks made of pineapple, etc. I was so busy I only had time for a sandwich. To my satisfaction the party was going with a swing when suddenly I noticed the room becoming depleted of guests. As there was a lull at the bar, I took the opportunity to go to the ladies. The scene that met me was most distressing. Vera for a start was lying on the floor feeling most ill, and there were many women in the same condition. I found out that the men were in the same predicament. Needless to say I was in the doghouse for a while afterwards, but luckily no real damage was incurred, although four soldiers, rather heavy drinkers, were in hospital for a few days.

I had a great admiration for the Italians; they have a talent and genius for creating beauty. I only wish that the whole world were endowed with the Italians genius for beauty and aversion to violence.

We went to the island of Ischia for a rest while waiting for a ship to take us home. Something had delayed the Anglo-Polish Ballet and they were not coming out to join us. Can you imagine this spectacular island with no holiday makers? It was paradise! We went to try out the famous mud baths but I hated it. I was a bit chubby for nineteen, and the big Italian women put me on a slab and with great gusto covered me with mud and cries of, "Bella, Bellisima!" I was left to dry, then hose-piped and put into an enormous marble bath with such hot water (my own fault, as I kept shouting, "Calda!" thinking it meant cold. Of course it meant quite the opposite; "Fredo" is cold). I hung over the side gasping for breath! There were also soldiers partaking of the baths. Vera severely reprimanded me, saying, "Disgraceful! What would those soldiers think? I could hear you screaming all over the building."

After this ordeal we went to sit in the natural hot volcanic springs, but there again I was unlucky, sitting and scalding my bottom on too hot a bubble. Feeling no thinner but extremely exhausted, I joined a party on a beautiful yacht. To my consternation they were all expert swimmers and immediately dived in from the side. It looked miles down to me, only an adequate swimmer who certainly couldn't dive, but on seeing Vera do a perfect swallow dive I jumped in quickly before being seen. The water was deep, horribly deep! The others even swam under the boat. To cap it all the meanies pretended to sail off and leave me! What a day! But worth remembering. While we lay on our beds in this so beautiful island we could hear the guns going off at Anzio beachhead. The windows used to rattle too. It seems that the island was used for certain young men to be sent if they needed a rest.

There's one incident that has a special place in my memory. It occurred in Italy when we were coming back from a party. As there was no room for us to travel together, I found myself sharing a horse and trap with a rather severe-looking officer, a dignified handsome man about thirty, very polite and correct. We drove in the moonlight along the coast, then we decided to walk for a while on the beach. The air was humid; we stood looking at the sea, which was calm, lapping ever so gently near our feet. I cannot resist water and suggested we swam; I wanted to swim. Without hesitation he walked a few yards away and took all his clothes off. I did the same we joined hands and ran in. As I sank into the black, velvety water, the phosphorescent sparks dancing around me, I was transported back to Aberdovey, swimming with everyone at Penhelig. I think we both for a while floated in our own small space. The world stood still, then we splashed and laughed and soon dried in the warm air. We never saw each other again and didn't even know each other's names. I cannot see any reason why hopefully when he returned to his family he couldn't tell them of his experience with, I suppose, that odd girl who wanted to go swimming!

Right from the moment I set foot on that train to London my adventures never ceased; in fact it's quite impossible to write them all down. I'm just trying to describe in reasonable order (with great difficulty) what might be of interest to you, the reader. Perhaps occasionally I also indulge in a little reminiscing for my own pleasure. In fact by writing this down I'm learning things about myself. What surprises me most is the fact that I actually achieved more than I realized. Despite my dreadful feelings of inadequacy due to my obvious lack of education and my extremely low opinion of myself, my behaviour was completely inappropriate. Enough of these thoughts. I've only reached nineteen; I wish eventually to return to the arbour at the age of seventy-eight. We've got a long way to go yet.

On the ship taking us from Egypt to Italy, which was much smaller and older than previous ships, there were many Polish people on board. We were told to be prepared for rather stormy weather. I noticed the stewards lifting sides up on all the tables, which seemed ominous, presumably to prevent dishes from sliding off. The weather did get extremely bad, but I went on deck and was amazed as our small ship seemed to be down in a hole with the sea up above us, then, shuddering slowly, the little vessel climbed until we seemed to be high in the sky, the sea miles below, then down we'd come again as if in a lift. As this continued, I found it…I cannot think of a word…perhaps breathtaking, certainly awesome. What was surprising was this tiny speck, this small vessel, gave off vibrations of confidence and strength as it braved this vast sea. I suppose this was partly due to the competence of its crew. Later we were told that the ship had been within a few miles of a cyclone!

On our return journey to England we were on a large and luxurious ship, where we shared a cabin with Kathleen Harrison, a great actress. She gave an unforgettable performance in a film with Emlyn Williams called *Night Must Fall*. Her famous line in it was referring to a decapitated body: "Grisly, that's what it was, grisly!" We all gave a show while on board in the lounge, where there was a stage and also a grand piano on which the well-known pianist Solomon gave a recital.

Kathleen gave a monologue, I did a Spanish solo. Vera and John Pygram danced a Tyrolean duet, which consisted of a great deal of clapping of hands and slapping of thighs. I thought their choice was rather strange, and as it turned out most unfortunate.

It was very much a together dance, impossible to perform on one's own—anyway catastrophe! Just as John leapt onto the stage he snapped his Achilles tendon, in fact we heard it go *PING*! Can you imagine poor Vera, slapping and clapping all on her own for about five minutes? No one pulled the curtain, the music continued and Vera looked like a mad marionette. She came off and had immediate hysterics.

On this ship I befriended a Belgian, Count Guy D'eutrement. Diana Gould was rather amusing, as she took an interest in trying to find a suitable partner for me. Heaven knows why. She was most impressed with Guy because his father was aide de camp to the king of Belgium. She also introduced me to the Marquis of Milford Haven, with whom I had tea, but her matchmaking wasn't successful as I didn't like the marquis at all, so Diana concentrated on my friend Guy. He was thirty-four and good-looking, but I don't doubt for one moment he was unbalanced.

Our relationship was strange to say the least. I was young and foolish, and I did lead him on, perhaps understandably as he looked and seemed a dream man for any silly young teenager. As usual I expected lots of attention but gave nothing in return. Well, I thought that to have fun and to be friends was good enough, but Guy became impossible as he was always craving for a kiss. Sometimes I felt a little bit like a snake must feel when the snake charmer starts his music. One such moment Guy got me at night on deck, and I was actually lifting my head up for THE KISS when I felt soft flakes all over my face. I let out a cry pleading for Guy to take me into the light. He dragged me to the gangway, saying, "More excuses! More excuses! You're driving me mad!" He did frighten me a little and I did know that by my foolishness I had bitten off more than I could chew. When he got me into the light I had a black face covered in soot, as the large funnel had let off a puff that landed on my face. I felt then that someone was watching over me. Guy did follow me as I thought he would, but

I hoped that Daddy and Mummy would help me to get rid of him. He became very difficult, talking to my parents for hours. One night Mummy and Daddy were walking in the garden, and Daddy said, "Kate, I've never seen you look your age before." Even then my father's sense of humour couldn't help but surface.

Now the wonderful part: on my return home the Anglo-Polish Ballet accepted as a matter of course that I was a member; I was told to rejoin the company for rehearsals after a short holiday. So Daddy, Mummy, Maureen and Rowland (who were now engaged) and I went to Moelfre for a week. We rented a lovely cottage where we had to climb a ladder to our bedroom. Moelfre Bay was near and full of miniature battleships, which I think were called Corvettes. Mummy for some reason really wanted to go on one.

One evening we all went to the village dance. Of course I danced with the young men from the ships, and with my usual shyness I told them of my mother's wish, so we got an invitation from the captain. We had a wonderful time. They had a miniature piano on board. Mummy played and I got introduced to pink gins. The funniest thing was that the lights were inserted in holes in the extremely low ceiling but some didn't have lights in, so the tall men were able to stand upright if they put their heads in these holes. That night the captain was given a message. It seems that they often had sort of alert practice to get ready to invade the enemy. The officers had a short confab, and as this was one of many they did consider keeping us on board, but the captain thought better of it, and sadly the party broke up and we said goodbye. Oh! And the captain sent Daddy a bottle of Canadian whiskey, as for some reason Daddy didn't want to come. The next morning when we looked out to the bay, it was empty; all the fleet of little battleships had gone.

THE INVASION HAD STARTED and we might have been with them! While at Moelfre the postmistress came with a telegram from Guy—a whole page of sentimental poetry. Of course Rowland teased me. I heard later that while Guy was waiting for a ship to take him home someone in a pub mentioned my name and Guy nearly wrecked the place. I mentioned how I would like to say I'm sorry to people in my past and surely Guy must be one. How do we know what he had been through in the war? A lot of men looked perfectly all right but they were hurt far more than we realised.

We all returned to Brookside, where I developed a severe case of mumps. I looked awful and, besides it being extremely painful I was a vision of head and shoulders with no neck. My appearance was not unlike the Elephant Man, and who should arrive but Lloyd, my New Zealand friend. My mother, oddly enough, had the same urge as Diana Gould, always trying to match me off to some man. In fact John Heaton first met Mummy and me on the bus to the airport, I showed some interest and Kate (as I often called her) straightaway asked him for tea. You know the rest!

When Lloyd arrived she got all excited, rushing into the bedroom, tying a scarf round my face so my distorted appearance didn't show, ignoring my howls of pain and my assurance that he was too good a friend to bother what I looked like. Lloyd explained that he had made a detour on his way home to see if I would marry him, the reason being his parents wanted him to marry his girlfriend as she was pregnant. It seems they had become extremely fond of her while Lloyd had been away at the war for four years. I was puzzled, never giving much thought to such things, saying, "Hasn't it taken a long time?" Lloyd replied, "For Heaven's sake! I'm not an elephant." After a small explanation about the facts of life, I, horrified, replied, "On no account do you go back till that girl is married. I won't marry you, but tell your parents I've accepted." They phoned us and that is what Lloyd did.

I recovered quickly, returning to the ballet company as a fully-fledged member, not only dancing the finale in *Les Sylphide* but dancing every part in the corps de ballet *Swan Lake* too. The ballet mistress found I had a gift for being able to step into any part without rehearsal, which was odd because I'm not really observant with other things. Lydia Sokolova, our ballet mistress at the time, was an unusual woman, sixty years old and on her sixth marriage to a handsome army officer of thirty-six. She had lost every hair on her body due to an illness. She had been ballerina in the Diaghelief Ballet, danced with Nijinsky in *Le Spectre de la Rose*, and also was the maiden in his ballet *Le Sacre de Printemps*. She taught us the original *Les Sylphide* as choreographed by Fokine. *Sacrifice in the Spring* was a nightmare of timing. I should know because our company rehearsed it with Nijinska.

I was progressing well, just the same as in most jobs one attains a better place step by step. It wasn't because I wanted to be a dancer, but I do have one thing in my nature which I know is good, and that is when I do something I do the very best I can, but as you will see as my life progresses, someone up there doesn't make it easy; in fact some of the obstacles placed in my way are quite annoying, some would say even horrifying.

We had a violinist called Guiter who had been Pavlova's violinist, playing the legendry "Dying Swan." I used to be enthralled listening to his stories of this ethereal dancer and her genius. He seemed to be most impressed by how she would stand in the wings an old woman (fifty was old to him), then she would float onto the stage a sixteen-year-old. When I asked his advice he suggested I did not go with the company to Italy but stay in London and study. I ignored his words of wisdom.

Let me for a moment indulge. Here I am on a blue-lit stage, the orchestra playing Chopin's Prelude; we're taking our places before the curtain goes up in *Les Sylphide*. I'm one of them, in a tight white satin (boned) bodice with tiny fragile wings, layer upon layer of soft white net billowing down to my ankles, and pink satin point shoes. My dark hair, which is long enough for me to sit on, is coiled up in the classical style, a small circlet of blue rosebuds on my head. I'D MADE IT! Excuse the crowing, but I'm reliving the moment! Who would have believed it?

Les Sylphides

I returned to Mrs Hamilton's boarding house, Notting Hill Gate, opposite the Mercury Theatre. I continued in the tiny garret in the roof, with gas ring and small skylight. I would listen to the young Germans flying overhead, thinking we would possibly be great friends in other circumstances, and of the futility of war.

While I was rehearsing in London Mr Moston, now major (or

something) in the army, Granny and Grandpa Alderley's neighbour, came to take me out for dinner. We went to Oddinnoe's Restaurant, a dinner dance! Edmundo Ross's Orchestra played. It was very swish and such fun! Mr (Major) Moston wanted to see me safely home, but I insisted he put me in a taxi. Unfortunately, while we danced an air raid had bombed Selfridges and obliterated the house behind Mrs Hamilton's. We were experiencing the V2, which landed without warning, much worse than the irritating little doodlebugs, the V1s.

Earlier when Daddy had visited me, I had taken him into the park, trying to show him a doodlebug, but his eyesight and hearing were so impaired it was quite impossible. It is amazing that my father, for all his physical drawbacks (being small and unable to see or hear), was so popular and was always sought after for his inimitable humour and wonderful after-dinner speeches. We sat on a park bench, me desperately pointing out doodlebugs (three, in fact) but to no avail, as he only saw the smoke when they landed.

I continued to go to class at Vera Volkova, rubbing shoulders with all the stars and struggling to attain a reasonable technique. No one could ever say I didn't try. I lacked confidence and had a low opinion of myself, but that made me try all the harder. Vera Volkova's pianist (what a pianist!) would collect the money. The name of any dancer unable to pay was listed in a book and you paid when you could! I was frequently in that book. Madame Volkova often told me to forget her charge. That's what the greats were like.

The ballet were rehearsing at the Stoll Theatre London, and during that time we got paid £3, half pay. There was a small Italian restaurant nearby and the owner, realising our predicament when we were very hungry and ordered only coffee with a roll, told us we could have (about four of us) a dish of spaghetti free every day.

I was and still am a little absentminded. One day the others sent me out to the shop. Between rehearsals I dashed out into Piccadilly with (luckily) my camel hair coat thrown over my shoulders (Maureen had got it for me cheap from Cleggs, along with one for herself and Mummy). A policeman stopped me, as I had forgotten my skirt! Piccadilly Circus was not the place to walk in knickers and high heels. The policeman was so nice. I was upset but he suggested I put my coat on properly and buttoned it up.

Actually the police were often helpful. Once I arrived in London late with no money, so the police found me somewhere to stay. This was the strange thing about my life: wherever I was, people were always friendly. No situation was ever unmanageable.

After a successful show at the Stoll, plans were moving for the company to go to Italy at last. Once again I boarded a ship, and of course things couldn't possibly go without some hitch, not if I was about. When everyone was allotted their cabins, there was a little problem because all the men were put together in one large cabin, the women in another, and the stars had separate accommodation. Good—except I had been put with the men! There was much laughter as they surrounded me; they said it was all right as far as they were concerned. Jasph Crandall arrived looking quite serious. He and his wife Mela Carter, the ballerina, our Swan Queen, agreed that I should go in their private cabin, Jasph taking my place with the men. This was extremely kind, as the voyage took weeks. Jasph would wake us every morning with an orange peeled and ready for us.

We danced in Rome this time, which was unforgettable, yet oddly it wasn't the Italians' singing that impressed me, but late one evening I was having coffee with Naomi Jacobs, the writer, when into the hotel lounge walked a Welsh choir straight off the plane. They recognizing Naomi and at her request they stood in front of us and sang full blast. Naomi was in tears; it certainly was a moment to remember, even for a nineteen-year-old. As Naomi remarked: "Something we shall never forget."

The first thing I did on arrival in Italy was to find out what had happened to Pamela. She had not returned to England as she'd wanted to stay with an American Air Force boy called Dudley, who was actually a really nice boy. I found her almost immediately and I was horrified. She had gone from a nine-stone glamour girl to about six stone, frail and unsteady but still beautiful, if anything more so, her big brown eyes looking larger and more velvety than ever.

She leant back on her pillows and started, "Dudley and I were together a lot after you left, then I became pregnant. Meeta, I was so scared. I didn't tell anyone, not even Dudley. I was put in touch with an Italian doctor, packed a bag and went to his private clinic to have an abortion. It was the most dreadfully frightening experience. They treated me like a criminal. They seemed so cruel. It was more painful than I can describe. They inserted what seemed like iron implements into me and then enlarged them. I wanted to die! I was so ill and no one sympathized."

I asked her about Dudley. It seems when she eventually told him it was all over, he was distraught, and also extremely cross with her for having the abortion. (Her story with Dudley continued, but that comes later.) I decided to get her into the company, which would enable her to get back to England. Having been a teacher, I taught her exactly what Konarski would give her at an audition. I also used some of my persuasive powers. She actually had a much better classical training than I had, and legs and feet any dancer would die for, but she was so weak it was an effort for her to stand, but she got in.

So the showgirl and the country mouse were once more united! We made an odd couple, she with her effing and blinding (she swore like a trooper), then there was me tutt-tutt-tutting. She was an awful girl with very little to commend her, yet I had a soft spot for my Pamela. Maybe it stems back to our need for companionship that cold Christmas Eve in the theatre foyer, sharing our tin of sardines. Pamela swore and copulated while still presenting the image of the perfect lady. We rarely went out together as my friends were different and usually a group. I had a lot of fun, but never stopped doing class, much to the ballet master's annoyance, who was compelled to take it.

I was slowly going up the ladder, having become now a devil instead of a witch, and one of the four little swans in *Swan Lake*. Many people of note came to see the ballet. One night the admiral of the fleet, Admiral Cunningham, was in the audience and later came on stage. He said he particularly liked little swans.

One night Pamela woke me roaring with laughter. Her explanation was, "I dreamt there was a queue of soldiers; you were measuring their penises while I was writing it down." I replied, "What's funny about that?" Her answer: "You doing the measuring!" Strangely we did not really have much in common, yet we worked and shared well together. One thing we did both enjoy was a drink. Both our bedroom and dressing room was always well-stocked with alcohol.

One day when we were resident in Foggia, Maureen's friend Henry Sutcliffe phoned. I arranged to go out for the whole day with him as Maureen had lectured me, "If you can see any of the boys we know, their mothers would be so grateful." Pamela lent me one of her frocks and supervised my appearance when a call came that Henry was waiting downstairs. After a rather formal, "How do you do?" (don't forget I was a little girl the last time he had seen me; I was always the little sister, never really seen but always watching and Henry would be about twenty-five) he produced a huge army coat, boots, helmet and goggles. I managed to put on all except the goggles. I was completely engulfed! Henry was more than six feet, the coat was below my ankles and I think the boots were size 10. By this time I had remembered that Henry's passion had always been motor bike racing, and of course he was a dispatch rider. I'd never seen such a big bike! He lifted me on to the back, saying, "Hold on, we'll do a run twice around the block." I think I yelled all the time but the engine covered the noise. "Fine, you're great!" exclaimed Henry and off we set at hundreds of miles an hour to Brindisi!

Pamela later told me she leant over our balcony hoping to catch a glimpse of us but all she saw were two soldiers on a terribly noisy bike racing around the hotel.

After about an hour and a half Henry stopped lifted me off and propped me up against a tree. It was so funny; I couldn't stand and slowly sank down. Even funnier, although I was supposed to be disguised, a lorry full of soldiers passed us and they all whistled. I suppose they were so frustrated with shortage of women their instincts were sharp. We arrived in Brindisi after, I think, about three hours!

He parked his monster of a bike in a shed, then, horrors of horrors, kissed me! I can recall that moment vividly, standing helplessly, helmet in hand, still draped in the large coat and boots, but it wasn't much to give to Mother's boy. He didn't ask for more, and seemed slightly embarrassed at his sudden impromptu gesture. He had arranged with an Italian lady to give me a room where I could resume my normal appearance.

Then we went to an enormous hut where I joined hundreds of army men for lunch. I queued with them and received a tin tray and tin mug. I think it was the usual corned beef and mashed potatoes. Afterwards we spent the afternoon on the beach and Henry related his story. "I was injured, and on a hospital ship when it was bombed, I found myself in the water with only my pyjama top. After swimming a while I saw a small boat coming towards me. I recognised the name on its prow. It was the ferryboat from Aberdovey. Of course I decided I must be delirious." It seems that Henry also had spent happy times at Aberdovey playing golf. Maybe it wasn't that actual ferryboat, but Henry swore it was. Of course every boat had turned out that amazing day at Dunkirk.

I never stopped working, doing class every day. If there happened to be no class I would work on my own. Now I think about it, I was doing really well. In fact as I write down my exploits, from the moment I stepped on that midnight train to London things went beyond my wildest dreams! Not only was I a fully-fledged member of this highly-thought-of ballet company, but I was now doing solos in the character ballets, moving up in the classicals too, and our little swans (Pas de Quatre) of *Swan Lake* had the reputation of being the best in the country.

I made friends easily, but one odd thing was the ballet mistresses, of whom we had two through the years, did not seem to like me. I don't think this was my imagination. The first one was Lydia Sokolova, a woman I admired immensely, particularly as she had been ballerina with the Diaghelief Company.

Helena Wolska, our second ballet mistress, was much worse with me. She would move me from one side in a ballet to another within minutes of a performance. Mind you, I could dance most parts without rehearsal. Fancy I was the girl that had galloped across the stage because I couldn't do the steps, now I could memorize all, although my technique still needed work. Wolska had also been with the Diaghelief and had fantastic lightness and ability. She was much younger than Sokolova and was dancing the Swan Queen. I was given the opportunity to dance my solo, the Ice Maiden. According to Pierre (whose criticism was acclaimed), it could have been a hit given the right help, lighting and so forth. But Wolska stood in full view in the wings eating an ice-cream cornet, and my lighting was pink, bright and deadly throughout. But as you might guess nothing deterred me; I worked all the harder.

One episode (which I feel should be told although I prefer it to be forgotten) was occurred when Pamela showed her true colours. We always locked our bedroom doors on going to bed, but this night when I had gone to sleep she went out without telling me, leaving the door open. I always felt this was not an accident, as she was often flirting outrageously with Konarski, who always accompanied "the Gorilla" Jan Cobel, the owner of the company. I called him by this name as he was a horrible hairy man, stocky with a long body, short legs, and very long, strong arms. He had a terrible reputation for tempting any girl with an offer of either money or a better part. I kept well out of his way, as no one crossed him.

I think Pamela let him know our door was unlocked to get him away from the watchful eye of Konarski, who for some strange reason seemed to guard Cobel and keep him out of trouble. What followed was quite horrific! I awoke to find the Gorilla on top of me, hot, sweaty, hairy, strong, all the time saying in extremely broken English, "More collaborassion! (That's how he pronounced it; it was a word he used frequently.) More collaborassion! And you be swan leader." I was on my way to being swan leader already without his help! I wriggled and struggled, gradually weaving my way downwards, eventually emerging up between his legs. Can you imagine a more awful journey? A horrible experience, BUT it could have been worse. Remembering the words of Grandma Carrie Alderley, "One cannot thread a bodkin whilst moving," I escaped into the bathroom, where I spent an awful night in the bath.

The next day the rumour was that Cobel had completely

flipped his top, attacking many girls, although no one mentioned or knew about my attack. There was a terrible row, but it seems Konarski dealt with the matter, hushing it all up. Cobel, I believe, went straight back to England. I never quite understood why, but there was tremendous loyalty between those three black crows, Cobel, Konarski and Demidetzki. I suppose most girls would have made a fuss, but it was unpleasant, and as it was dealt with without my getting involved, I quickly forgot it (in fact until I started to write my story I never gave it another thought).

I hadn't as yet flown in a plane. When I mentioned this to an American airman he immediately arranged to take me one morning to the airbase. The name and the place evade me completely, but it was probably near Foggia, definitely northern Italy. Strange how important things like the place or date escape me, yet I remember stupid things like as we walked to the jeep some men were playing football and the ball hit me! I never liked ball games. I was never any good at them and always seemed to be the target (l think I mentioned my sister was good at tennis, also table tennis, even though she wore glasses, being extremely short-sighted—a pity because she had beautiful eyes).

Back to the American airfield. The first part is hazy, except I vaguely remember going in a sort of tower to watch the planes arrive, and there was a suggestion that I would have coffee with some of the crew when they landed. Then all hell broke loose! Three Liberators were coming in to land from a mission, but they all had damaged undercarriages. It seems that this type of plane was extremely difficult to land. The first one crashed on the airfield, bursting into flames, and within seconds the second one did the same. There was absolute pandemonium, so I was forgotten and wandered amongst the carnage watching these men helplessly hosing the debris with that awful foam. All seemed to be crying without any control. I felt somehow remote, even criticizing their futile efforts as they tried to carry the blackened lumps of flesh, which were far too hot to pick up, so they kept dropping them. Within another few seconds the third Liberator crashed. This time all I could see was a plume of smoke about a hundred yards away. I believe the Liberator carries a crew of nine men, so within a few minutes I perceived twenty-seven young men killed.

On a lighter note, we had a dancer with us called Mouse Lambert. I believe her father was Constant Lambert, the conductor for the Sadler's Wells Ballet. She was not interested in being a good dancer; her one ambition being to find a husband. She was so keen that sometimes her ambition was almost embarrassing. Eventually she found the right man, but to all our amusement he had a most unfortunate name: Capt. Peter Hole. She then became either Mrs Mouse Hole, or Mrs Pee Hole!

I haven't mentioned my romantic activities so far, because as far as I was concerned there were none worth mentioning. I had many friends, some obviously intending to become more amorous than I, but on the whole most seemed quite happy to take me out to marvellous places, etc., with no strings attached. To mention a few in Italy: there were my Americans, then there was one young English officer, the Hon. St. Clair Wheeler. I remember teasing him because he was good-looking but wore glasses, and when he took them off he squinted. Eventually he got a W.R.E.N., who we both agreed was better for him because she was more amicable to his needs, but because she was jealous he had to end our friendship. While we were together we had fun visiting the Vatican and the Coliseum. He was a bit odd. He talked about his flat in London painted all black, which made me a bit apprehensive.

Me and friends

Then there was another English man, the one who had a great deal to do with the opera in Naples. He always gave me the royal box and I took my dancing pals with me, but he became a nuisance. I decided it wasn't worth the hassle just for that privilege. Actually, maybe I was a little odd, because one man asked my friend Vera could she stop me from persuading him to take me in a gondola. It seems he said he would not be responsible for his behaviour! When I wanted something I was a real pest!

Vera Dawson was a good friend, a far better influence than Pamela I'm sure, but she shared rooms mostly with Eunice. Vera was an only child, often, maybe in a rather spoilt fashion, reminding us of this, sometimes giving the impression of being slightly snobbish, but she was basically good and kind, often coming down from her high horse with a bang, with such incidents as the rats choosing to eat her knickers and no one else's.

There was also the time when she proudly arrived with all her expensive leather luggage embossed with her initials in gold. This was rather unfortunate as the whole of Italy had posters up for the troops saying BEWARE OF V.D. Luckily she was able to add the letter L. to represent her second name, Leslie, although it always looked a little crushed. She and Eunice were most proficient dancers. When I had stood in the wings with the dwarf in Lewisham, it was Eunice and Vera I had seen posed together as white sylphs in that blue and heavenly *Les Sylphide* that extraordinary evening when I looked upon a scene that was, and should have been, beyond any hopes I entertained. "You'll be lucky if you get into a third-rate chorus"—the words of that agent echo in my mind. The great Volkova's verdict was no better, yet here I was only one year on, dancing with these talented girls.

I think I've regressed in my story as usual. I'll never get to the age of seventy-eight at this rate. There's so much more to come; as I write so many things pop up that I had forgotten. Each memory makes me realize I wasn't such a dumbo. Even if this never goes into print, it's achieved one aim: giving me more confidence, although my behaviour sometimes is nothing to be proud of.

Once when Joyce Gearing, Vera Dawson, Eunice Gibson and I were having tea, we made a sort of pact that we would never marry Poles, probably because of Cobel's behaviour, which was unfair because the Polish people are a fine lot. Anyway, our pact went up in smoke; we all married Poles, and only one had anything to do with the company.

Vera was the first to succumb to their charms, becoming friendly with a Polish airman, which led to an unusual happening.

One night about two a.m. Vera began to have hysterics. As she was not the type to behave in this manner, this caused great concern when she became uncontrollable, screaming and fighting with the girls. This continued for quite a few seconds while they tried to calm her. Her friends thought it so strange they took particular note of the date and time. Later it was found that her airman had crashed and as he was coming down he cried for Vera. He luckily survived but lost a leg, and they married about five years later, not long after my own wedding (to a Pole). Vera was one of my bridesmaids.

While all this was happening to me in Italy, Mummy and Maureen were both busy driving in the MTC. Maureen had also done a spell with the Civil Defence. The flat at Brookside seemed to suit. We owned the ground floor, and Judy and George Turner (he was the doctor) owned the flat above, and Detective Limbert and wife were at the top. Sadly Granny and Grandpa Alderley had lost everything in the Blitz and were now living in what I can only describe as poverty. They had a small part of Auntie Peggy's house in Chretian Road, only five minutes' walk from us over the River Mersey. What seemed awful was Granny (Carrie) seemed to have some sort of kitchen on a small landing where she seemed in a terrible mess, but as always made the best of it.

It was getting time for the company to return to England. I must say I loved Italy, and whilst there I saw most of the operas in Rome and Naples. Once again we found ourselves on a return ship. This time the Black Watch were returning too, most glamorous in their dark green kilts, or better still trews! I was goggle-eyed at such handsome men. But then it was decided they would teach four girls the eightsome reel to entertain everyone in the lounge. I think the idea must have come from there being three expert Scottish dancing girls in the ballet; I was the odd man out. We were dragged out of our cabins at an unearthly hour to practice on deck so nobody saw us, as it was to be a surprise. I have never worked so hard in my life. It was so difficult! Those young Scottish men were absolutely brilliant (so were the three girls) but on top of this problem that I had to overcome, they treated it like an army manoeuvre. After my feet had tried to beat, spring and do steps I didn't even know existed, I hated the sight of those gorgeous men. I also had Eunice watching me with a look of horror every time I raced off in the wrong direction. It was, of course, an enormous success.

Back home I was at last to dance as a soloist in my hometown with the Anglo-Polish Ballet, having some really lovely dances to perform. Of course I was extremely excited. Relatives and friends were coming to watch at the Palace Manchester! Now here comes an example of the many obstacles I mentioned. The week before this amazing step up the ladder, the bridge of my nose began to swell. By the time we got to the Palace my nose was twice its size, tight red and painful, and when lowering my head the throbbing and pain was bad. What could I do? I shadowed the sides of my nose with makeup and performed as best as I could. Everyone knew I was dancing but couldn't recognize me. Back home at Brookside I was flat on my back looking like, as my mother reassuringly said, Ally Sloper, a horrific character of a man with a huge nose with masses of warts on it. In fact I had a carbuncle with exactly twelve heads, which Mother triumphantly counted while poulticing. I was by this time quite blind. George, the doctor from the flat above, was a good friend; his wife Judy, a beautiful willowy blonde, was also in the MTC. George cared for me, as it seems that having such a thing on my nose was quite dangerous.

Slowly, after many weeks, I began to recover. I was able to see with one eye, and with a large dressing on my nose I wobbled unsteadily into the garden to entertain a young army officer whom I knew in Italy. I managed to get to the table, but then my nose seemed to explode blood, not particularly attractive! As my parents were out, Capt. Reeves helped me back to bed. To give him credit he later gave me a miniature cut-glass vase, which I treasure, putting one snowdrop in even to this day.

Eventually I returned to the Anglo-Polish Ballet. I worked hard, gradually getting all my old parts back, solos, little swans, etc. Also I got to dance the role of the wife in "Mathew is Dead" (*Umarl Maciek, Umarl*). One of the black crows actually remarked it was the best rendering of the part he had seen, which was flattery indeed as Alicia Halama normally danced this part. I was really making progress!

There was more talk of the company going abroad again. As we had lost our rather aggressive wardrobe mistress, I had the brainwave of getting Mummy the job. First I asked Daddy's opinion. Although he hated her to be out of his sight, because he was such a kind, delightful man he agreed immediately, realizing what a marvellous opportunity it was for her. I spoke to Cobel and the next thing we all, including Mummy (I shall call her Kate from now on), were being inoculated against all diseases to be caught in India and China! Kate, of course, could do the job better than anyone. As I said before, she could do anything if she wanted. To top all this talent she was still, at the age of forty-seven, most beautiful, often attracting men of twenty. In fact one young man aged twenty-two took her out regularly. The funniest thing was she even took the attention of the beautiful Pamela's admirers.

Mummy and admirers

Although Daddy did ask me to watch her, there was no need. She was popular and enjoyed herself, but was never promiscuous, the reason being she was just not interested. She was brilliant but passionless, the only thing I seem to have inherited from her without the first part. I certainly loved men, but the minute they became excited I seemed to switch off like a dead duck! Good thing in a way as it saved an awful lot of problems.

While we were waiting to go abroad we could go to any show in London free. Two friends of mine were the principal dancers at the Windmill Theatre. They booked me a seat in the centre at a special rehearsal for officers in the forces. In my stupidity I had no idea what the Windmill was (a nude show, in case you're as daft as me). I sat happily right in the centre of an all-male audience. Imagine the row's amusement as they stood up to let me get to my seat. When the show started, Michael Bentine, the resident comedian, was so vulgar (well, what parts I understood), then my friends appeared with a corps de ballet. They gave a pretty performance; their costumes were lavish, different shades of purple velvet, the lighting effectively coming from the glass-tiled stage flooring. As they ended, horror of horrors, all their bosoms popped out of their bodices, and all the cameras in the audience went click! I couldn't believe my eyes. In those days all nudity had to be static and cameras were banned, but this obviously was a special. I don't know how I got out of that theatre! I don't know why, but my ignorance often caused my friends great amusement. Perhaps I was too busy trying to get somewhere; I was mostly in cloud nine.

Of course the first thing I did on returning to London was to attend Volkova's classes in West Street near Cambridge Circus. How to explain this amazing centre of activities? Later it all moved, I believe to Covent Garden. Any dancer of note went there. It existed of two floors, filthy dirty, classes going all day, take your choice. The classes were given by brilliant teachers whom I got to know by attending most. There was Gongarov, the grumpy Russian, who never hesitated to whack me, and Anna, lovely and kind but we felt she was inclined to give us heavy legs. She was popular with the dancer Violletta Prokofiev, a lovely girl who had escaped from Russia and became a star with the Sadler's Wells, married an Englishman and changed her name to Elven, thus enabling her to work and stay in England. Then of course there was Vera Volkova. Their music was provided by the best pianists who were able to improvise or read marvellous music to whatever the maestros choreographed. We danced to Beethoven, Delius, Chopin, etc., and also fabulous music was composed there and then. The feeling of the class was so enjoyable it was an honour to be part of it. Many celebrities would come to watch. Epstein the sculptor was one. As he was creating his monstrous *Adam and Eve*, it doesn't say much for our physique!

The media talks a great deal about the partnership between Margot Fonteyn and Rudolf Nureyev, but they should have seen Margot when young, with her partner, the handsome Michael Somes. They often rehearsed after class a pas de deux under the expert eye of Volkova. They took one's breath away. It's impossible to put into words the feelings vibrating from this remarkable partnership, the immense sexual, vibrant tension. Yet as soon as the music stopped the spell would break and they were once again just two professionals striving for perfection, which they were lucky enough to attain.

Two other dancers who had this extraordinary gift were Alicia Halama and Konarski, who at one time had danced their very famous but simple "Shubertiana" at the Palladium London, which brought the show to a standstill so great was the applause. Halama and Konarski were an exceptional pair, choreographing and dancing such brilliant ballets as *Crakow Wedding*. They performed "Mathew is Dead," "Dancing Woman," "Preludium" and also "Faust." Alicia Halama always kept very much to herself, always looking perfect. Once we were travelling by train and I accidentally walked into their private carriage, which was full of Poles, the Gorilla, Konarski (his watcher), Demidetzki, an overpowering smell of cigars and garlic AND Alicia Halama with a brown carrier bag over her head. I did notice, in that split second, slices of salami sausage disappearing under the bag. It seems Halama thought the trains dirty, and this was the way she kept her makeup immaculate!

Konarski was as handsome as Halama was beautiful, and he was also similarly remote. Pamela chased him disgracefully but he remained aloof, until one night he seemed to succumb and arranged to meet her, having presumably escaped the watchful Halama, but to Pamela's disgust and frustration he was unable to perform, owing to the boys of the company getting him impossibly drunk. I often wondered whether Halama arranged it; Pamela never got another chance.

After our classes in West Street, a group of us would walk to Valerie's Patisserie, where we would talk and partake of her wonderful aromatic coffee and hot, freshly baked croissants. Valerie was famous not only for her coffee house but also for the marvellous tortes she made. They were not like our cakes, but they were marvellous, mouth-watering creations, different colours and flavours, layer upon layer of very short pastry, all butter I'm sure, divided by buttercream then decorated beautifully depending on what flavour: lemon, orange, coffee, chocolate, etc. We could buy them whole. You can see I loved my food.

I've lost the thread a bit, having stopped writing for a few weeks. So I'm back in my arbour with my glass of Chablis, trying to regain the memories of years gone by. Why not a spot of philosophy while I take breath? I've learnt rather late something that might be useful to others. Working hard at whatever opportunity is placed before one is not always the right thing; often valuable time and energy is wasted. This was my mistake. I never stopped to think and consider the outcome. My advice to others is sit down with paper and pen and work out what they really want in the future and how they can get it. Don't waste precious time; life gets even more exciting at seventy. Prepare for it!

It's so lovely here! I wish I had the gift to bring your senses into this green haven with me. I'm so lucky! The views in this dappled sun are quite breathtaking: my small garden untidily rampant with flowers and scent; beyond and slightly lower, the farmer's field, green and lush; the sheep grazing; oak trees laden and lolling; further still the mountain Tal-y-Fan. The peace is only occasionally disturbed by the raucous distant eruptions of the farmer swearing, which somehow increases the feeling of tranquillity as my cat purrs happily beside me. I built a pond with sparkling fountain, waterfall and underwater lights. Wonderful! But quite ridiculous: not only does it get full of leaves from the oak trees, but it's only about three feet deep and five feet wide. It does, however, give me lots of pleasure (except for one day when I managed to fall in it). While the cat watched (as always), I leant over to rearrange something and promptly fell in headfirst. To my horror I managed to submerge completely with an odd feeling of disappearing down a black, silent gulf. Eventually surfacing covered in mud and very shaken, I managed to struggle out. Not wishing to take the mud in the house, I stripped completely, gathered my clothes together and stuffed them into the washing machine, which happens to be directly opposite the door. I then went and sat naked in my bedroom which adjoins the kitchen. Within seconds my delightful postman walked in and placed my letters on the table, calling, "Hello!" If he had been a moment sooner it does not bear thinking what would have met his gaze. I came out of this incident with nothing more than a large black eye and a little more sense (one's forever learning). No arranging of the pond unless empty.

Back to the past. About nineteen forty-four Granny and Grandpa Alderley had two girls in the forces billeted with them. They were sisters, name of Sawyer, one in the army and one in the WAF. One instance makes me realise how times have changed. One of the sisters was upset because she had left some sanitary pads on the table. Granny reassured her, "Peter William wouldn't know what they were, he's never seen them." What a difference to today, when they are advertised on the television! How times change! Grandpa was stone deaf and Granny made a hearing aid. This she created from an old flexible gas pipe and a funnel, and instructed him to put one end to his ear. The idea was to speak down this, but the WRAC poured his tea down it!

Although our families were sometimes in dire circumstances they never failed to see the funny side and laughed whenever possible. There were many amusing situations. Grandpa loved to play Bridge, and they had two friends called the Brewsters who came every week, quite ordinary people except for one thing: their conversation. It went something like this: Mrs Brewster, "Your bid, Beautiful!" or, "Oh, but I did, Beautiful." The answers were usually, "You stupid woman, that's wrong," or, "Idiot, what are you doing?" What made this funny was Mr Brewster was round, red-faced and bald, the ugliest man, a little like an overblown Captain Mainwaring from *Dad's Army*. His wife, on the other hand, was an intelligent, quiet, unassuming woman. She drove their rather large car while he was the worst possible backseat driver. My father could not contain his impish humour.

One night he placed bottles and tin cans so that when Mrs B. backed out of the drive Daddy pulled a string, releasing the cans and making such a racket. Mr Brewster, while giving his usual nonstop directions, thought they had crashed, but Mrs B. never turned a hair. He nearly exploded.

Granny and Grandpa were funny during the game too. Granny would get quietly irritated with her spouse. Thinking he couldn't hear, she would murmur, "Peter William, you're a fool!" Peter William would perk up, saying, "What's that you said, Carrie?" The answer was always in a gentle voice, "I only called you a noodle te tumps." They were a delightful couple, he six feet four and handsome, and she forever charming even when her patience was stretched to the limit, which it frequently was.

The Sawyer girls' parents invited me to stay with them while I was rehearsing in London. They were extremely kind to me, but sadly I became seriously ill with pneumonia. I found out later that the doctor had ordered them to poultice my chest and back twice a day. Mrs Sawyer was too nervous to apply this hot thing so they both performed this ritual together, Mrs Sawyer carrying it and Mr Sawyer applying it. It seems I became delirious, screaming and accusing them of burying me wrong way round in my grave. Mrs Sawyer suddenly realised the window frame at the foot of my bed resembled a cross, so she promptly closed the curtains and I became calm. This was just one of the many hurdles I encountered on my struggle to achieve something. It was rather like a game of snakes and ladders. One thing at least every time I climbed up I did go a bit higher. (I had gradually worked my way up from witches and bridesmaids, the lowest of the low, to solos in the character ballets and little swans and swan leaders in the classical.) I gave up my flat with Mrs Hamilton, the knickerless landlady, who was thinking of retiring anyway. When I left she gave me two lovely watercolours of Paris and London.

Eventually Mummy (Kate) and I were on a ship heading for India! One night I had another of those magical moments when I was alone with one of the dancers, Johann Florres, a half-caste young man of dusky colouring.

The moon shone on the deck like a spotlight. He started to dance. First he clicked his fingers, then he began to beat parts of the ship with his hands and feet, eventually moving all over the deck, even up the sides and swinging on the ropes of the lifeboats. I watched this fleeting figure leaping about so rhythmically that music seemed to be present. Sometimes he would grab me and whisk me around and then return to his own fantasy. It was quite extraordinary, sadly only seen by me!

Our first performances were at Kalyan, a garrison theatre. Nearby was a fairground where Ram Gopal, the famous Indian dancer, was performing.

There also was my favourite thing, a big wheel, but this was like none I had ever seen before being turned by hand! We had only been in this place a short time before the dancing boys played a trick on me. I woke one night to find a large snake across my chest! It was so big my two hands could not span its width, but it was not as I imagined a snake to feel; it was warm and friendly. The boys had borrowed it from the fair.

After a few weeks we left for Bombay, where we were to stay for quite a long time. Kate soon had the wardrobe organised, everything ironed, mended and on its hangers. She was able to make the most of her great adventure, taking photographs and visiting all the places of interest. A pity I didn't do the same, but I was busy trying to improve during the day and partied late after the shows, busily going up the ladders and sliding down the snakes! My mother did occasionally try to get me out with what she considered eligible men. I did have my men friends, but that's what they were, good friends, and we had fun.

In India they had marvellous tailors, their little shops opening onto the street so you could see them working on their sewing machines. They would make a frock in a few hours, costing very little. I took them a parachute, pure white silk of course. A pilot gave both Pamela and me one; she got a red one. I wore the frock that same evening to a dinner dance. Actually I went out with some Marines at Mummy's request, but I very rarely went out with less than two men at a time as it was more fun and led to fewer complications.

In Bombay Pam and I found ourselves in wonderful and unusual accommodation, a large, airy room with a balcony and the strangest but exotic bathroom that resembled a tree house attached to our bedroom. There were wooden steps at the back of it so the servant could enter to clean. It contained a tin bath and a shower and lovely little lizards looking down on us with huge dark eyes. At first we left our room in the most awful mess with knickers and stockings strewn everywhere, but when we returned from a late show and the dining room was closed we would find food in our room, and everything would be tidy and washed! It was rather like having a fairy godmother. From then on we were tidier, but it was a long time before we saw our guardian angel, who was a dignified family man of about fifty named Mohamed.

One performance Pamela and I were waiting for *Sylphide* to start. As we were ready in our ballet frocks we sat with our skirts over the back of our seats so they didn't crease. As always Pamela was smoking, something that was absolutely forbidden, as ballet net is known for being extremely flammable. One dancer, I think her name was Carlota Grisi, about one hundred years before had burned to death. We both were drinking gin (I did have some vices in common with Pam). Anyway there we sat like two angels, dainty wings quivering and blue wreaths on heads, drinking and smoking, when suddenly I noticed in the mirror a sheet of flames.

We very quickly got out of our frocks and stamped out the flames. Kate came to the rescue and supplied us with new dresses, and managed to hush the episode up.

Everyone was supplied with boiled water in old Gordon's gin bottles on our dressing tables. Kate dashed in one day very hot and thirsty, took a huge gulp of our real gin, and gasping with shock promptly fell backwards onto our skip basket, where she was all legs and arms.

Another Kate episode was an hour before we were due to perform the ballet *Swan Lake* and our headdresses had been mislaid. Kate confiscated our cotton sanitary pads and transformed them into elegant swan's wings, which we wore with dignity (I hope).

On the whole performances went without a hitch. I did on one occasion bruise my big toe rather badly and the nail came off. As I was unable to perform the little swans' point work without it, I stuck the old nail on with plaster while the new nail grew. One night while having dinner with a young man I suddenly remembered the cleaners were going in at midnight, and I had left my toenail on the dressing table. I shrieked, "My toenail! My toenail!" Eventually, when my escort realised the reason for my panic, he rushed me back to the theatre, only to find that the meticulous cleaners had dusted and replaced the disgusting nail!

We eventually embarked on what can only described as a most unusual and exciting journey on a train from Bombay to Calcutta. It took days and nights and was very hot and very uncomfortable, but Kate organised our carriage. She put a blanket on the floor, which seemed to help with the dust, and arranged to supply us with tins of grapefruit juice, fruit, and a tea boy! At this time there was terrible trouble in India and we saw quite nearby the fighting, particularly at night with fires and shooting. Kate took many photographs as we travelled along.

On arrival half of the company stayed at the best hotel, the Grand, and the other half in a hostel. Some complained, but I don't know why because our accommodation was even better than the Grand! I should know, because I became friendly with the owner of said hotel, often having dinner with him. This again was a strange occurrence looked on with amazement (and I've no doubt jealousy) by Pamela and other glamorous members of our company. He and I were really quite unsuited, and yet we got on extremely well. He was about twenty-six, wealthy, intelligent, sophisticated, Indian of course but light-skinned. We would sit in the dining room of his hotel, and I, nosey as usual, would ask, "Who's that?" and "Who are they?" He always laughed but always explained, "That's my English secretary; she looks after my young son, my paperwork, and also my other NEEDS! Up on the balcony watching, they are my female relatives."

He was good-looking. In the evening he always wore a white jacket with a high collar with eight buttons, each of which consisted of about eight large diamonds. Once I had lunch in his beautiful apartment and he showed me a glass case with another set of these buttons. I said, "Oh! Can I have one?" I remember him being amused, saying I would have to do something else for those, but then, serious, he explained they were family heirlooms. He took me to the famous Two Hundred Club, where I would often see Cobel and Konarski drinking champagne too.

It was at this time that I made the biggest mistake of my life. I was twenty and still trying desperately hard to succeed as a dancer. One night, sitting on a step with my ballet master, I had a rather strange conversation, completely out of place. Jasph, the unapproachable master—an odd man, handsome, fair-headed, introvert, and dreamy—who never seemed to be with one, for some reason confessed his marital problem. It seems that although he and Mela Carter were seemingly devoted and inseparable, her demands on him were more than he could cope with. Fancy choosing me for his confessor—gauche, inexperienced, one who spoke first and thought afterwards!

After his embarrassing revelations I decided to be brave and ask him how I could improve my dancing. His answer in his drawling, soft American accent was "Virgins are always lacking in emotion, honey!" As usual, without thinking, this stupid, gullible young woman rushed off to find a man! I chose the most eccentric homosexual extrovert, one of our dancers, a talented man well advanced into his thirties, with a few army officers always in tow. Why did I choose this man? The answer is I don't know, except perhaps there was a possibility he wouldn't accept. No chance of that. He needed little encouragement.

I can still see that dark, large room with its hard bed. I had sunk my boat, given my word, and there was no escape. But let me be quite truthful, he was in no way to blame and behaved as any normal man. The whole hideous episode ended up with me crying and pleading for him to leave me alone.

That evening was to be the last in Calcutta. Everyone went out. I had been asked out for dinner by my wealthy Indian friend, but I was nowhere to be found! My homo friend, after trying to dissuade me from going out, tricked me and locked me in a room where no one could hear my cries till it was far too late. I was distraught, as I had promised and we were to board the ship the *Ascanias* early that morning. I took a taxi to the Grand hotel at about seven a.m., barged into my startled Indian's bedroom and blurted out my apologies. When he got over the noisy awakening, he said I was not to be upset, that he would get in touch in Manchester as he might be there to buy the Midland Hotel! Of course I didn't tell him what had actually happened, except that I had been locked in. But I did tell Jasph Crandall, who was horrified, saying he was only joking!

Too late! No more sex for a long time! India had been an exciting country, a mixture of old cultures rubbing shoulders with the new, Eastern magic and mystery quietly enduring the European invasion. It's almost unbelievable but the next thing Kate and I and the company were on the ship *Ascanias* bound for China.

I think it was on this journey that I found my cabin a little hot, so I managed to get a hammock erected on deck, where I settled myself for the night, curlers and all. At dawn I woke to find my face level with a soldier standing to attention with his rifle. He explained, "The ship has docked, and as there are Japanese prisoners of war working on the docks, rather than wake you they put me on guard. Would you like a cup of tea?" He then appeared with a large tin mug. I lay there supping and chatting, and as I relate it now, I realise I'd come a long way since teaching those babies.

Hong Kong. What can I tell you? Exotic! There was Repulse Bay and its masses of huge, beautiful flowers and glorious water, and two large sort of fairs, I think they were called little and big worlds. They were not like our fairs but places full of open stalls selling wonderful food. It struck me as being very clean. Then there were dance halls reminiscent of the Ritz, with rather an odd group of Chinese girls whom one paid to dance with! My dreadful mistake, my downfall—in other words the man I suppose had been my lover—got up onto the stage and sang! We were always friends and I tried hard to forget my experience, but I suppose you have realised it still haunts me.

I really enjoyed the food in Hong Kong. I found a wonderful restaurant near the theatre that served lobster, which I loved. But whenever I found anywhere I liked it seemed to be banned the next day as when I went back, there was always a notice "Banned to the Armed Forces," and that included me. I never really found out the reason. One possibility could have been the forces' behaviour.

There were one or two occasions I remember in Italy, with some colonels swinging on the chandeliers. Another time I was sitting on a balcony having a meal with a Canadian when below on the ballroom floor some RAF men lit a fire and proceeded to do a war dance round it. Agreed, sometimes I did see men getting a little out of hand, including high-ranking officers, but who could blame them? They were often in horrific situations, and knowing that worse could come they had reason to let steam off!

Forgive me, but I must retrace my steps back to a magnificent hotel in Calcutta, India, called Firpos. How could I have possibly missed it out? I visited this grand place frequently. It was memorable for its sweeping staircase, huge chandeliers, and opulent and hushed grandeur. I would ascend this magnificent staircase and seat myself in the restaurant above, where I could watch from the balcony any distinguished visitors arriving. I must have looked an incongruous figure, usually having just finished morning class. Tired, dishevelled and hot, my dusty ballet shoes tied by their ribbons to my old practise bag, I loved to sit behind an enormous coffee meringue and a goblet of iced coffee, much to the amusement of the attentive waiter who seemed to know what I wanted before I ordered. One of the reasons I so enjoyed this indulgence was that it reminded me of the many times Granny and I would go to the Premier Cafe in Cheadle Cheshire, where their speciality, and Gran's favourite, was meringues! She did so love them, and certainly couldn't afford them. I wished I could have taken her to Firpos. She would have stood out with her dignity and charm.

Actually her daughter Kate wasn't doing too badly as she often was also there. I usually didn't embarrass her with my presence, but on one occasion there was a terrible rumpus from her table.

I was amazed to see my mother screaming and prancing about with her skirt held high, everyone getting a good view of her knickers! It seems a large horrible insect something like a hornet had gone up her leg. She soon recovered under the soothing attentions of her escorts. I couldn't help feeling smug because things like that were usually my problem.

It was about this time Kate had one of her infrequent motherly moments. I got an order to come down from my bedroom immediately and join her in our lounge. As it was only inhabited by us, without giving it a thought (something I do frequently) I descended in my dressing gown minus one eyebrow and curlers in as I happened to be practising my makeup for the performance. My poor mother was mortified as she had ensnared a gorgeous blonde man, pianist to the Goons! Actually he did take me out and we had a laugh about the incident. In fact he took me to rehearsals where I listened to a marvellous jazz band, Ella Fitzgerald singing, and an ugly little man who played the double bass. It was as big as him; he would twizzle it around especially for my benefit.

Pamela and I continued to share dressing rooms and bedrooms. Maybe a little of my determination to improve brushed off on her as she was now a passable dancer in the corps de ballet. I hope none of her habits brushed off onto me, particularly as I remember one instance. I was resting in bed as there was no show that evening and Pam had gone out. It must have been about seven thirty when suddenly Pam appeared looking absolutely immaculate, and rather too dignified! She introduced me to what seemed a nice young man in the Air Force, asking me would I entertain him for a few moments while she freshened up. She then made a most dignified exit into our bathroom.

Mark and I were left and soon got chatting happily, Mark

making himself comfortable, feet up on Pam's bed. Don't forget we were only in our teens, possibly he was a little older. I poured him a drink from the cabinet between us and time passed. Suddenly we realised that more than an hour had gone by. Horrified, we saw water seeping under the bathroom door! Mark got the door open and what met our eyes is hard to explain. Pam was lying with her feet up on the toilet, her knickers round her ankles, her beautiful hair full of sick, unconscious! For once I didn't know what to do. Mark took complete control (I do love men!). He ordered me to mop up with everything I could lay my hands on. He undressed Pam, put water in the bath and dumped her in it, washed her, put her in her red parachute nightie, put her in bed, and then proceeded to help me with the mopping up.

Suddenly I heard a strange noise from the bed; Pamela had pushed the sheets back and lifted her legs up to her ears! I, in an absolute panic, raced and caught her with the towel and a foot at each ear. By this time I was crying with exasperation and helplessness. Believe it or not we managed to get everything back to normal and Pam asleep. Mark, so kind, reassured me that it was nothing to do with me, and I was not to blame. When I think back to this awful episode, here was a young man who could have been disgusted with such a horrible situation and just left me to deal with it. Let's face it, it was not his problem, but we set to as if we had been friends for years, both of us bare-footed. I remember tying my skirt up and he rolled his trousers up. Pam was certainly a liability.

The next morning I told her it was time we discussed her behaviour and perhaps did something about it. She then started to go back over all the men she slept with. I think even she became worried when we completely lost count! I did try and advise her. She, on the other hand, used to try and advise me on my gauche ways and appearance. Since my carbuncle my nose had become rather Grecian; anyway her advice was, "You could be quite beautiful if you had your nose done, and when you're in a hurry do you have to run upstairs using your hands?" It was quite true: when the stairs were steep I sometimes, without thinking, used all fours!

Eventually it was time for the company to leave for Singapore. We were given, rather unusually, the choice of either travelling by luxury Sunderland flying boat or the longer route on the ship the *Salween*. As I still hadn't flown I chose the plane; my mother chose the ship. She had a marvellous voyage, travelling with our manager Capt. Rood (good name!) and our orchestra; in fact she was the only woman on board!

Her album is full of photos of the journey. Of course my trip went all wrong. For some reason there was no room for Pam and me on the luxury flight, so we ended up travelling on a Dakota, which had a rather bad reputation for crashing and was called the sardine tin!

Everyone else left early, and then later we embarked on what looked rather like a khaki dustbin. We sat all alone, being the only passengers except for the pilots. We seemed to be in one large cavernous space, on seats that were unattached to the floor, which was most uncomfortable as we dropped down innumerable air pockets. Also most reassuring was a huge mound of parachutes, which we had no idea how to use!

We eventually arrived at Saigon, which was being used as a transit camp, where we were to spend one night. As we climbed out of the plane I found it difficult to walk; later in the shower the floor seemed to move, but except for this all was well. We spent the evening playing skittles made of old wine bottles with the men waiting to move on. The next morning we set off again in our sardine tin on our rickety chairs.

How am I going to describe our stay in Singapore? It was quite different from any other country we had been to. The climate for a start was very humid and warm, and difficult to dance in. It was at this time that I began to feel unwell. We stayed in an ENSA hostel, which sounds awful but it was quite the opposite, an interesting building situated in a large, beautiful garden with a magnificent fountain as its outstanding feature. I have a photograph taken by my mother of Mela Carter, our Swan Queen, posing in an arabesque on the side of this fountain.

Four of us had the whole top corner of this building, which was completely surrounded by a covered balcony that overlooked the fountain. It was so warm at night we moved our beds, mosquito nets and all, onto this balcony. As usual we had the small green lizards with their large, liquid black eyes watching us from above, and once a not-so-welcome scorpion sat under my bed and I had to call for a servant to deal with it while I kept my feet up. As I mentioned I was beginning to feel ill. Sometimes I felt all right, then I would feel dreadfully tired. I got an awful abscess on my neck; when that went every gland in my body began to hurt. I never knew we had so many places with glands.

One night I was in such distress I got into a bath of cold water, which seemed to help. This really doesn't seem to make sense now. Why didn't I get medical help? There's no answer, except that I kept feeling all right, so continued dancing and practising. Then all my teeth began to hurt and my gums to bleed! This was a horrible experience for me as I vowed I would rather lose a leg than my teeth, a saying which later made me wonder whether some unearthly being wasn't having some sort of game with me. I did this time rush off to the army hospital, where they told me that I had probably got poisoning from the black residue left in my saucer from the lead teaspoons. Their advice was to rub my gums with salt. Thankfully it worked, but unbeknown to me the poison was still working around my body, waiting! I was at this time being escorted out by a young naval officer called Christopher. He did propose but as usual a friend was all I was prepared to accept.

We went to many parties held by the governor of Singapore. He made us most welcome and let us use his pool whenever we wanted so long as we allowed the large resident toad to join us!

My mother got on so well with everyone, and as she was so beautiful mixed easily on all occasions, except once when things went slightly wrong. There were three young men in the Navy waiting below in the hallway. One of them was very good-looking and Pam was very smitten, so she asked Mum and me would we mind keeping the attention of the other two. We didn't care so long as we had a nice evening, so Pam pointed out to my mother which one she wanted to herself, but my mother quite innocently got the message wrong and the handsome young man spent the whole evening with her. Pam had to make do with a boy that she didn't like at all.

The company eventually came to the end of its commitments and we were to rest until there was transport to take us home. But I was restless, maybe because I was not well. Anyway I agreed to dance with a small company called London Calling, run and starred in by a man called Duggie Harris, a middle-aged comic who did female impersonations. One number he was dressed as Carmen Miranda and sang "Coffee in Brazil" while another girl and I stood on either side of him wah- wahing! We had on beautiful Cuban dresses and played the maracas! Sadly one of my maracas flew off and hit my partner, who seemed to think I had done it on purpose! I also did a solo cancan, landing heavily every night on my left knee, which seems to have saved my life.

It's no use, I have to own up: I think I've got one of my countries in the wrong order since looking through my mother's album, but it makes no difference of importance, so I'm not going to rewrite this just for a matter of a few thousand miles.

Eventually it was all over and we were to board ship and head for home. It was to be the most fabulous voyage, as the ship had been a large luxury liner full of rich holiday makers. But now, even better, the war was over and the ship was full of men and some women returning home. On the lower deck was an empty hospital and hundreds of men. I decided to go and watch a film on the first night, a coloured Betty Grable picture. As it began my leg started to ache. I asked the rather high-ranking officers in front would they mind if I put my foot up near them. That was the last thing I remember. There were fleeting moments of people speaking as if in a fog, such as, "Quiet, she's extremely ill."

I had heard of red lines on one's body when poisoned and thought it was a fallacy, but on one of my conscious moments I saw on a pillow a large lump of grey, blue and black—my knee—and running from it up my leg two brilliant red lines! At first I could feel nothing, which I believe was when I was at my worst. I was lucky that about two or more specialists and doctors were also returning home. As I was the only patient I got excellent treatment. It seems they referred to me as Princess, and decided to give me penicillin.

One hazy moment I surfaced and heard them say, "If she doesn't respond, it will have to be amputated at Port Said, we have no facilities on board." Strange, had I made a bargain with someone over my teeth? Luckily a few days before we came into port I began to improve. My goodness, then I felt the agony! As I became more comfortable I really learnt what had been going on. A young red-haired Catholic priest had been seeing me, as they obviously thought I needed one. Why a priest? I've no idea! It seems when his services didn't seem to be necessary anymore the matron had difficulty getting him away.

The hundreds of troops on my deck had been following my progress from day to day. Unbeknown to the strict matron, they had had a watch on me through the windows on their deck and bulletins put up for all to read! Then as I grew stronger I got a visit from a funny little rotund TOCH man in uniform. He wore large, very thick glasses and proudly entertained me with his repertoire of gramophone records. It seems I made his day, as the troops had not really appreciated his war efforts.

The next thing was when we stopped at Port Said and there was great excitement with the Gulli Gulli man, etc.(I never did find out what he did.) As I was improving, I was left alone while everyone went on deck to watch the fun. Suddenly at my windows appeared the cheerful faces of as many troops as could fit. They wanted to know if there was anything I wanted and threw lots of roses onto my bed. I remember being afraid in case they touched my very tender knee.

I was now able to read the many letters everyone in the company had written encouraging me to get better, the strangest one being from my homosexual disaster suggesting we got married!

There were just a few days left before we arrived back in England. I had missed all the fun, and fun there had been. The war was over, something worth celebrating! Mummy had had a marvellous time, having found three excellent Bridge players, and dancing and drinking was in full force. One Army officer had taken a liking to me (whom I didn't happen to remember), as it seems he'd spoken to me just before I had passed out. He asked the matron's permission to carry me to the upper deck to the last party. I clung around this man's neck as he struggled up the massive staircase, terrified of touching my knee, even my foot! Everyone made me comfortable so I could eat drink and be merry too.

Poor Daddy was so upset when they carried me off the ship. I think both he and Maureen were there to meet us. Mummy stayed for a while with the company as agreed in her contract. Surprisingly I recovered quickly, returning within a few months, possibly a little too soon as my leg was still a bit weak. This time I did not have to start from the bottom of the ladder, but in a way this was not a good thing, as the vicious Wolska, knowing my weakness, asked me to dance the wonderful pas de trois from *Swan Lake*. Of course I had to refuse as my left leg was not ready for such extreme exertion.

We were to rehearse in London for a few weeks before going on a tour of the British Isles, replacing our leading dancers with Loda Halama, Alicia's sister, and Enone (Talbot) and Toni Repetzki, husband and wife, excellent classical dancers. We had some good bookings ahead, such towns as Cambridge, Oxford and Bath to name a few, and were to play to full audiences. All seemed well and I was getting stronger all the time. Loda Halama for some reason took the day off at a moment's notice and I was asked to dance the bride in *Crakow Wedding*. After only one rehearsal with the awful Wolska, who as you can imagine did her best to not instruct me, I performed the leading role.

I suppose I should have been amazed and thrilled at my good fortune, but it was all wrong. I wore the star's dress, I believe I looked beautiful, and after the performance Pierre invited me for a drink into his dressing room—hallowed ground! He congratulated me on a performance, which he said he recognised as star quality. The next day I went into a hotel and three gentlemen walked up and said, "Madame Halama! We so enjoyed your performance yesterday." It didn't get any better. My pay never improved, the audience were obviously not told of the change, and Loda never took a day off again. So to me it seemed as if I had gone up the ladder only to slip down the snake once again.

At this time the management seemed to have great plans for the future of the company. Rehearsals were in progress for a new

Spanish ballet *Carmen*. Enone was an expert Spanish dancer, and Llalagia, a well-known exponent of this genre, was employed to choreograph and instruct us all in this new and very expensive project. You can imagine the excitement and enthusiasm running through the company. New ballets were to be performed in fantastic costumes; in fact some of the old ballets were to have a facelift also. *Swan Lake* was one of these; the four little swans were to have tutus instead of the long ballet skirts. Cobel was going to relaunch the Anglo-Polish Ballet with no expense spared!

We castenetted, postured and stamped wildly with great hopes and gusto! One of the new productions was to be *Sacrifice in the Spring* by the great legend Nijinsky. His sister Nijinska rehearsed us; we crawled in a crocodile with our heads tucked between the sometimes smelly male legs in front for hours to the interminable boom-boom-de-boom of Stravinsky's music. I'm not surprised Nijinsky went mad. It wasn't doing us any good!

Norman Stride, an odd young man, rather insignificant except when he got on stage, was a super character dancer, and his famous advice was, "However you dance, give them a snap finish and you're bound to get applause." He was immensely thrilled, as he was to be the bull in *Carmen*. Sensibly he requested the bull's costume to practise in as he and Llalagia had worked out some interesting movements in his dance.

This was when we began to suspect that things were not going too smoothly. Something was very wrong! When the bull's costume arrived it had to be carried by two men, as it was impossible for less. Head, horns, torso, jet black with red eyes, completely solid and immovable, this dreadful thing was dumped on the stage, massive and menacing! At first we couldn't help laughing until we saw Norman's tears. These so-called brilliant costumiers had also sent our new *Swan Lake* outfits. We all rushed to try them on, but to our dismay however we struggled it was impossible! We just couldn't fathom it out until Kate solved the dreadful mystery. All the measurements had been reversed! Chests and busts were around 18 to 24 inches, waists were 35 to 44 inches. The extravagant material—velvet, satin, tulle, sequins and rhinestones—was all wasted. Even Kate couldn't rectify this catastrophe.

Nothing came of any of our hopes. Cobel, I presume without the watchful eye of his good friend Konarski, had, I think, been conned into spending an immense amount of money, leaving the company with nothing to show. We had had a successful tour of the British Isles playing to full houses, but we needed those two new ballets and those new costumes, and nothing came of it after all our hard work.

As the company was to have a long break before starting again, Jasph Crandall offered me a retaining fee. Would you believe it? This was the very man who had first taken me on three years before. I refused as I thought it would be a good idea to take a temporary job. According to everyone it was exceedingly difficult at this time to get work, but I saw an odd advert in a magazine: "Ballerina wanted for Kilburn Empire, good wage." As usual in my ignorance I applied and was accepted. The owner, a huge man with a huge cigar, said that I would give his show a touch of class! He offered me my own star dressing room, and most important a very good salary.

Mela Carter lent me two of her beautiful tutus, and I got the whole front row for Jasph, Mela and some of my friends from the company for the first night! The rehearsals were so strange. I was left to devise my own steps and present a large, elaborate gold frame where the other girls posed in their everyday clothes. Imagine! On the night when I finished my pirouettes and the curtain parted in the picture frame, the girls of course were nude, except for such things necessary to describe the scene: hats, masks, pram handles, illustrated Easter bonnets or Little Red Riding hoods, etc.! My friends were convulsed with laughter and

I was mortified. Once I got over the shock it was a most enjoyable experience. I spent most of my time in the other girls' dressing room, which about six of them shared, and they told me some marvellous stories.

It was about this time that Pierre died and Pamela became desperately ill with tuberculosis. Why? I don't know. It could have been her lifestyle, her chain-smoking, or possibly she caught it from Pierre, with whom she danced in the ballet *The Cow That Spoke*. Norman Stride, incidentally, was a brilliant cow.

I went to see her in hospital. Pam had had a lung collapsed in an effort to heal it. Of course smoking was forbidden, but there she was with fag ends she had found and was smoking them stuck on the end of a hairpin under the sheet! She was also up to her usual amours with any male willing. It seems that Dudley, her boyfriend, had tried to get her to join him in America, but owing to her illness she was unable to gain access. I never saw her again and many years later I heard she had died.

While working in class I met Peter Fiske. How can I describe Peter? He was a strange boy, kind, considerate, wore gloves during class, good-looking and known as a philosopher. He was quite a capable dancer but also had a wheelbarrow on which he sold secondhand books in Cambridge Circus. He was about twenty-five and owned a house in Neal Street just off Cambridge Circus, a rather tall, dark and ominous building three or four storeys high. He was a terrific conversationalist and knew many different and interesting people. He introduced me to Valerie's Patisserie in Soho, where after class we would drink her wonderful coffee and eat croissants straight from her ovens. Other times he would take me to see some of his many friends.

One I remember particularly was a drama teacher at a college in London. She was unusually normal compared to most of his friends, about fifty years old, seemingly most upset about a much younger male colleague who was just introducing new and modern writers and successfully getting rid of Shakespeare from their programme. I wish she could have seen into the future, say fifty years ahead, her beloved Shakespeare and even Chaucer became even more popular than in her day. Mind you, I think she would have been disgusted at some of the modern work.

Peter told me if ever I was stranded I could stay with him, so one late night I ended up at his door. Peter was not at home but a boy called Bambi let me in. Bambi had this odd nickname because he resembled a faun out of Disney's famous film. He was beautiful, blonde and willowy, a male replica of Pamela, but more evil! It was his eyes that resembled the creature the most, large and dark, almost all consisting of big black irises. His lashes, again like my friend's, were extravagant, which all contributed to his similarity to the said animal. He was homosexual, fascinating and hypnotic, having slightly the same effect on me as Guy. As we waited he began to caress me. Suddenly a voice boomed out from overhead, a strong, authoritative, well-educated voice, "Take your filthy hands off that young girl." I stared unbelievingly up at my benefactor, guardian angel, whatever! She peered down from what seemed to be a double ceiling with a wooden ladder leading up to it, a bit like a small gallery, only hidden. This, I discovered, was the Countess Eileen De Visme, and this was where she lived!

Peter arrived, and after Eileen had described Bambi's behaviour Peter evicted him and took me and my suitcase up to his most private room, where I think few were allowed. What met my eyes I shall try and describe. It was a large room with a gigantic bed in the centre that seemed to be a mattress draped in black satin, with two huge Chinese sort of dogs that burnt incense. Around the whole of this room were books of every conceivable kind. I stayed with Peter free for many happy months. There were rules: a black bolster was placed between us and I was not allowed to cuddle. The wonderful part was every night Peter would read while the incense burnt, Sanskrit, Madame Balankiere. None of this I understood, but then there was Edward Lear, Dickens' tales, and Aubry Beardsly. I lapped it all up.

The Countess would take me to the Council Baths where I would lie in a great white porcelain bath with one chrome tap the size of a pudding basin. The big fat washerwomen would take my laundry, which I was supposed to wash myself, and it would be all clean and ironed before I had finished my ablutions.

Sometimes the Countess would take me to Oxford Street. Standing still, she would announce, "Look at them, Meeta, where do they think they're all going in such a hurry? They'll get there soon enough. Why rush?" Another time she showed me a 1924 magazine, *The Lady*, where there was a picture of her as debutante of the year.

Peter and Duggie Harris (of *London Calling*, the maraca fiasco) sometimes took me under the Thames at Wapping to an old pub that was said to have been frequented by Dickens. The only drink available there at that time was barley wine, very nice too! There were sometimes a few fights but my two escorts took good care of me. Duggie was, I suppose, an odd companion for me. He was about forty-five and nearly always wore a cap with the three monkeys—see no evil, hear no evil, speak no evil—on it. I did hear a rumour he had been to prison. Sometimes he took me to the Cafe Royal, where according to him we sat at a table Oscar Wilde had frequented.

As we were only about two minutes' walk from West Street I attended classes morning and afternoon, so of course my money ran out, but my technique must have improved. It was time I found work. Sadly I heard that the ballet had deteriorated, so I looked for something different. If you attended the classes you always got to know about forthcoming shows and auditions. The Glynbourne Opera wanted classical dancers for the opera *Orfeo* by Gluck. Work for dancers after the war was sparse, so the auditions were packed with hopefuls, especially if it happened to be something special, and Glynbourne was very special. I presumed my chances were slim, but went just the same.

I entered the large room feeling rather small. The pianist was well-known, Dimitri. He smiled with encouragement and I stood before the master-to-be, Rupert Doone. There was no problem and I knew instantly that Rupert liked me, so I didn't need to dance! I later learnt that this was nothing to do with ability; the man was bonkers! Sad but true. As was normal procedure before commencing rehearsal, dancers had a short class. This was when we began to realize that things were not quite right. At the barre Rupert asked us to do rond de jambe en l' air DERRIERE. Anyone who's a dancer would find this a little odd, even today. Normally one performed circles in the air at the side. Try doing it behind yourself! Then the next shock: the first rehearsals were to be of the "Elysium Fields" (Heaven). Rupert told us to walk about thinking of nothing, which we did for hours while poor brilliant Dimitri played, and Rupert sat crossed-legged sucking his thumb. He reminded me of a new potato dressed in jeans. It was weird. When we eventually went to the cafeteria for lunch we felt really odd, still in a daze. Why didn't we question it? How were we to know? Choreographers could be most peculiar, and Glynbourne was known for only hiring the very best, sparing no expense.

Next came "Hades," which was much worse. Except for me most of the dancers were really brilliant. Rupert had them doing the most awful things. The women performed as lesbians. Poor Enid Martin was a perfect example of a Royal Ballet member who in those days was easily recognised as she wore a sort of uniform: always impeccably dressed, long earrings and very ladylike! Rupert had her standing in a full plie in second—in other words legs apart and knees bent—while one of the boys came out from between her knees bearing a lantern! This scene was the last straw! We didn't mind the obscenity so long as we learnt some steps, but after weeks we knew nothing.

The boys formed a committee and complained, but worse was to come! I watched all this with trepidation, and decided to take the bull by the horns. I went to Rupert on his dais and asked him what he wanted me to do. His answer, "What would you like to do?" Thinking quickly (not my forté), I answered, "Can I roll about the floor?" And that's exactly what I did in "Hades," for the whole scene, getting absolutely filthy, but it was quite fun because I just rolled everywhere watching everyone working hard. My part was the only original Rupert Doone choreography left in I think.

The artistic director and producer Carl Ebert called everyone to rehearse on stage together. Imagine his horror when we all stood saying in all those weeks we had learnt nothing! Don't you think this resembles my experience with *The Merry Widow*? Most odd. It was dreadfully sad. Here was a full company of brilliant dancers in a fantastic opera with unbelievable music, orchestra, singers and scenery, not to mention an audience of famous people and critics, and there was no time to learn anything. We didn't dance. Carl Ebert, just as Cyril Richard had done, moved us about the stage, and very little dancing was performed except in the "Elysium Fields" Peggy Sager and Paul Hammond worked their own dance together.

One morning when Colin and I were on the train to Brighton going to one of our dreadful rehearsals, I couldn't bear the thought of two hours of rolling, so I suggested to Colin we played truant and went swimming. We did, me in my black knickers and bra and Colin in his underpants, which I remember were striped! By about lunchtime I phoned Glynbourne and spoke to Rupert, telling him I had felt faint and Colin had stayed with me. The owner of Glynbourne sent his Rolls for us. Although the other dancers knew very well what I had been up to, they were most forgiving, and anyway I did have the dirtiest part! Carl Ebert had great vision for the spectacular, and in "Elysium Fields" I was sent up white steps without any handrail! My arms uplifted sixty feet above the stage, and there I stood on a platform about three feet square, which was most effective, but there was no dancing and it was a bit nerve-racking.

The details of the opera I can actually remember clearly. It was a simply marvellous production. Artists would be brought from all over the world. Conductor Fritz Siedry, Orpheo sung by Kathleen Ferrier, Euridice was Ann Ayers from America, Amor was Zoe Vlachopoulos (Greek). During the interval I would have to bathe (I was very dirty). The bath was situated under the window overlooking the gardens, from which I could hear Joyce Grenfell, Noel Coward, and many other famous people enjoying their picnic lunches and Champagne. In the next room I could hear Benjamin Britten playing the piano while Peter Peers sang. I thought it was an awful racket, but that's just my opinion.

Sometimes we would all have tea in the beautiful grounds, where many famous people would join us, Benjamin Britten of course discussing his music, Frederick Ashton his choreography. He was in charge of the dancing for *Peter Grimes*. Why couldn't we have had him? It was just my luck to get a madman! That's ungrateful, because Rupert hired me and Fred probably wouldn't have. Not to be unfair to our master—it seems he had been a brilliant dancer and well thought of—but it was just most unfortunate that our production had not checked Rupert Doone's life over the last twelve years. It seems that many years before he had been invited to perform in a charity performance in the lounge of one of the largest hotels in London. His audience consisted of many notable people. In the front row (I was told) there sat some legendry ballerinas such as Karsarvna and Sokolova. Rupert raced into the centre of the floor, and before the startled gaze of these famous old ladies with their elegant fingers poised on their teacups, he began a grand pirouette en l'air in second. This is when a male with his leg at 90 degrees hops round at top speed, then draws his foot in, causing him to spin numerous turns—a wonderful spectacle, except Rupert had nothing on. Not a pretty sight! The audience clapped politely. He then disappeared into a home and was not heard of again until the Glynbourne hired him as our ballet master. His name was kept on the programme and he sat placidly watching our final rehearsals, and nothing more was said.

While the opera was in full swing everyone started to talk about a fantastic new project. Powell and Presburger were planning to make a film all about a ballet company and call it *Red Shoes*. Every dancer in London wanted to be in it. There was to be more than one audition. One girl said to me, "It's useless, only the best will be chosen," so I packed my rather old and tatty practice clothes and joined the elite at one of these auditions. As usual I felt out of place (I always did). The vast rehearsal room was seething with dancers.

Alan Carter (ballet master) attempted to get us all at the barre to warm up, which was quite impossible; we were so close together we were touching each other! At the top of the room was a long table with about four people who had to choose about twenty-five of us from the masses. Robert Helpmann seemed to be the man in charge, while Alan Carter stood at the side keeping us in order, rather like a sheepdog with his sheep. We were told to pose turn across the stage one at a time. This was to be the extent of our audition! I cannot remember exactly what I did but I know it wasn't what they asked for. Robert Helpmann stopped the procedure and asked me, "Do you know the classical ballets *Swan Lake, Sylphide, Giselle*?" I had never danced *Giselle* but of course answered, "Yes, I've done them for four years."

That was it, I was in! This time there was no messing, as everyone knew their work. Alan Carter was brilliant ex-soloist with the Diaghelief Ballet, his famous part being that of Harlequin. I introduced Peter Fiske and Norman Stride (The

Cow) to him and they also got into the film. On the whole things went smoothly, but there were some mishaps. Our costumes were fabulous, the white frothy ballet frocks for *Giselle* quite beautiful, but the frilly knickers were attached to the bodices. We stepped into this outfit and were laced in tightly, then a lot of high stools appeared, very high! These the stage hands lifted us up onto, the idea being that our beautiful dresses would not be creased! On our feet were brand new pink satin point shoes. We just looked like a row of fairy dolls BUT we were not! The first thing was I wanted a wee! The next thing was my feet, as they hung two feet above ground, began to swell, so I took my shoes off (why was it always me?).

The next minute our cue came to go before the cameras. Of course I could not get my shoes on. I can see Michael Powell now, fuming because this delay cost a fortune. But I think they did begin to learn that dancers do have special needs. The stars also had problems, two worth mentioning. The great legend Leonide Massine, who played the shoemaker and also acted as our stage ballet master (I thrill just to think of it now), in one part was expected to sissone, chasse, sissone, chasse, assemble, double tour three times across the stage. One double tour is quite a feat, and Massine at the age of fifty executed this once impeccably. Because the lighting or something was not perfect Massine was asked to repeat his performance; in fact they had the impertinence to ask him to repeat it for a third time. To their astonishment Massine coldly refused.

Another incident was when Lludmilla Tcherina burst into tears after repeating her fantastic steps in her ballet, how many times, heaven knows. The producers were surprised to see her ballet shoes soaked in blood. Gradually they began to learn how to treat us.

During this time Eunice Gibson had kindly let me share her top flat in Hammersmith. What happy times! We would sit in our beds on Sunday morning with our tea and toast listening to Alistair Cook's *Letter from America*. Fifty years later he was still doing it! The first day I was paid at Pinewood studios I had never had so much money. I sat on the bed throwing it all over me. I don't think Eunice really approved, but I never thought anyone really approved of me. She was and is such a good friend and a brilliant dancer. Her Scottish solo in the "Divertissement" was a gem.

I felt I was making good progress up my ladders at last, particularly when given a small movement in front of the cameras. I was dressed as, of all things, a South Sea maiden. My outfit was most exotic, my long hair decorated with hibiscus similar to my "Coffee in Brazil" when I threw my maracas about! It seems that the technicians actually asked for the rushes of my scene be repeated, which I was told was most unusual. The press also came. They placed me on one of those high stools, took photographs and said I was to be on the front of *Picture Post*. Surely at last I had reached the top of a ladder.

The next morning I arrived early and was stopped by the actor Anton Walbrook, who played the part of the impresario in the film. What followed seemed most odd. I had never spoken to him up to this moment. He was sitting on a seat playing an instrument like a mandolin. He stopped me and started on a long and incomprehensible lecture. I still cannot fathom why or what he was up to unless someone had asked him to break the news to me; whatever the reason he was not up to the job.

After I had stood listening politely for what seemed ages, I eventually realised he was telling me not to be upset because of disappointments. He never did say what. I found out later my moment of glory, so admired by the technicians, had been scrapped and was lying on the cutting room floor. I was of no more interest to the press; my photo would not be appearing on the front of *Picture Post*. I hated Anton Walbrook after that. What did he know about disappointments when I had just slid down the longest snake in my attempt to get somewhere?

Some cast members of Red Shoes: *Presburger and Powell on the left, Moira Shearer centre, me behind her right shoulder, Massine second man from right in black.*

When the filming came to an end I found I had enough money to take Volkova's advice and just do class, at least for a few months. I went back to Mrs Hamilton's, where she gave me a really nice basement flat, and I decided to give myself one last try. During this time I was asked to do a charity performance in Lewisham. (That's odd for a start, back to the place where it all began!) But it never seemed to dawn on me what progress I had made.

Mela Carter was to dance *Le Spectre de la Rose* and I also did a pas de deux with a boy called Phillipe Perrottet and the pas de trois from *Swan Lake*. This was most exciting. I would wear a diamante and winged headdress and a beautiful tutu, and was to perform the pirouette, the other girl the beaten steps. This meant that the male dancer, who incidentally was to be the star of the show, would be supporting me. He was arriving from Paris that day and would only have a short time to practise.

I, of course, was thrilled, having no idea who this great star was. He arrived on stage with just fifteen minutes to practise supporting me. It was then I knew who he was: THE DEVIL FROM FAUST! Rovi Pavinoff, the man whose legs I had crawled between and ruined his magnificent pirouette! Of course I said nothing but pretended to be most efficient. With my mouth dry with fear and his hands on my waist I sissoned and chassed and pirouetted across the stage, finishing with as many turns as he could push me round, ending with a great flourish and applause! Jasph Crandall came and said he was surprised how good my classical effort was, once again too late. Quite funny: at the end Rovi received a bouquet, not us.

So here I was at Mrs Hamilton's, having used nearly all my money. Christmas was approaching and Maureen called to stay one night on her way home. She and Rowland so wanted a family, but there were problems due to her being so ill as a small child. She had come to London for some sort of examination. That night she was taken seriously ill. I had only one bed so of course I was on the floor. We got no sleep, and at one point she asked me to sing to her. I was so worried all I could think of was "My baby has gone down the plug hole," which seemed to soothe my poor sister, but looking back I realise it was most inappropriate.

As the night went on Maureen got much worse and to our horror began to spit blood. We were both so frightened, but I knew that in the flat above me there lived a young doctor, though I had never met him, and it was by about three a.m. I ran up the stairs and knocked at his door. Doctor Bell appeared dishevelled in his pyjamas. I did notice two women on his bed. He came immediately and promptly got my sister into King's College Hospital. It seems she had caught an infection in her throat. She was dreadfully ill and I visited every day.

Eventually she began to improve and I took her some grapes, one of which I peeled and placed in her mouth. She said later she didn't like to grumble but it felt like a walnut with the shell on! Daddy was so grateful to Doctor Bell he was actually lost for words of thanks when he met him, unusual for my father. I was determined to get Maureen home for Christmas so I managed to get her out of hospital sooner than they recommended.

Even though she was very weak, she didn't want to spend any longer in my flat than necessary because of her dreadful experience (a pity because I loved my little flat). Anyway we decided to go to the local cinema, which was showing *A Christmas Carol* by Charles Dickens, one of the best films made of it, with Sir Seymour Hicks as Scrooge. We had to queue and an awful drunk woman came and sang to us. (To make matters worse she began to wee, and weed and weed, continuing to sing.) The next morning I bought a goose and we went to Euston Station. I wanted to go for our tickets so I asked Maureen to hold the goose. Her answer was, "I feel too weak to hold the ticket!" Poor Maureen, but at least we got home on Christmas Eve!

When I eventually got back to London, even though I had spent those months and money on just training, I seemed to have lost that urge to climb those ladders. I went to David Paltenghi and he gave me a part in a television show. We performed a musical by Beverly Nicholls at the Alexandra Palace. In the finale

I was a prostitute in Paris, short black tight satin skirt, very high heels, swinging a red handbag. At the end of the show the gendarme was to kiss me centre screen; of all the men in the show I didn't like this one! Worst of all, when he kissed me no one bothered to tell us when the camera was off, so the embrace went on forever!

After this I continued to do class, not really knowing what to do next, when a Polish dancer called Jan pleaded with me to go as his partner in a small Polish company that consisted of only eight members: Machnic, the manager, who also played the violin; Kazik, driver, stage manager and pianist; Luda, soprano; Meesha, contralto; and four dancers, two boys, two girls—Eurick and Yadja, Jan and I (who was now renamed Meeta Thomasievich!). None of them spoke English except for Jan and Machnic a little. They toured the country entertaining in all the places, camps, etc., where many Polish people were. Quite a few were mining or in forestry camps.

Our accommodation was excellent but sometimes we found ourselves in large Nissan huts on camp beds, with all the women in one and the men in another. We never knew from one week to the next. Of course the Poles were naturally of volatile natures, which led sometimes to hilarious moments. One night we were to entertain General Sikorski. It so happened he was late for the performance and was to catch a train after the show. Machnic, our manager and also violinist, decided to play our final Mazurka faster while Kazik continued to play at the correct speed. We didn't know which to follow and so some danced fast and some slow, hence utter chaos! Heaven knows what Sikorski thought!

Kazik (short for Kazimierz) was about thirty-two and a delightful man, perhaps a little old-fashioned, with everything so correct, a lot of bowing and clicking of heels. All the Poles had these manners; sadly, after a while in England they soon shed these mannerisms, although they continued in their own company,

Polish clubs, etc. Kazik had been offered a place in a conservatoire of music somewhere excellent, but his father had wished him to continue studying at university to gain a degree in economics.

This all came to an end when the war started. He was a lieutenant in the cavalry. I don't know where the horses came in but I know that Kazik hated riding the beasts. He did tell me about learning to jump with a parachute, which he disliked as much as the riding. Anyway it was a waste of time as he was in the front line and taken prisoner almost at once. When we later married Kazik put in our photograph album a photo of him aged 25, in prison with his identity number on his chest, and next to it a picture of me at the same time, aged 14, sitting on the wall at Aberdovey.

Polish P.O.W.'s Orchestra, wearing outfits made of paper

He told me little of his experiences but I did learn that they were not pleasant, and yet he told me they were not all bad. At the start he put his identity papers in his mouth as the men in his regiment were being shot. I have pictures of him and Machnic in their orchestra, clothed in evening dress made of paper. They and their musical friends busied themselves giving lectures and concerts. The Germans supplied them with the best instruments, that was the good part. All their bunks were down to about two planks as other men spent their time burrowing tunnels in an attempt to escape. The ones who did not occupy their time frequently were found hung in the toilets.

Food was terribly short, especially toward the end of the war. Kazik said the German guards were as hungry as they were, or even worse. One particular guard for whom he was sorry exchanged bread for German cigs. And now here was Kazik, after a spell back in uniform in Italy, in England, like so many unable to go back to Poland, touring with this strange motley of artists entertaining his people, hardly any of whom spoke English, many not knowing what had happened to their families, all most distressing.

A short description of my companions would be a good idea, each of them interesting characters. Machnic, about thirty-five, was a brilliant violinist, good-looking but with a hasty and over-excited temperament (this nervousness due, I'm sure, to his imprisonment). Eurick, in his twenties, a dancer, from what I could gather had lost his parents when very young and wandered the streets of Warsaw begging. (My memory is vague at this point but I think he mentioned the Resistance.) He was a tall, immensely strong young man, humorous, kind and most conscientious. He was Yadza's partner and they danced cabaret numbers such as the Apache Dance (something I longed to try), while I and my partner were the classical pair.

Yadza, Eurick's partner who looked old and hardened, danced her part well, but one never could get friendly with her. Meesha, contralto, graceful, with a beautiful voice, was middle-aged, pockmarked, and very plain, but from her manner you would have thought she was a beautiful teenager. Polish women were inclined to "minny" (my word) when men were about, which made me squirm. The men's attitude and manners toward them, all this kissing of hands and adoration—don't get me wrong, I liked it, but didn't like how it affected the women.

Loda, soprano, what a character! How do I describe her? A blonde, blue-eyed bimbo with a voice like an angel. As we trundled along in our ambulance she would sometimes sing, once a never-to-be- forgotten rendering of "Ava Maria." She was terribly short-sighted with extremely thick glasses, but was too vain to wear them; because of this she ended up doing some really ludicrous things. She was a terrible flirt but as she was unable to see, often her behaviour toward the strangest things was quite funny. I think it was quite possible for her to "minny" in front of a cow with a hat on.

One of her problems was wanting to "pee-pee," as she called it, at most unfortunate moments. One time when waiting to make her entrance onto the stage a pee-pee was necessary. She looked around in desperation and saw the vase of flowers in front of the usual statue of the Virgin Mary (these small shrines were always near). To my horror she took the flowers out, pee-peed, replaced the flowers, crossed herself and swept onto the stage.

Jan, my partner, was young but did not stay long with the company. He was inclined to be too amorous. Sadly I complained and I think Machnic and Kazik sacked him. They then asked me to get my own partner, Freddie, dancer from the Royal Ballet. I was lucky and Freddie joined us with little persuasion. He was an excellent partner, but was most unfortunate. Right at the beginning of our tour he obviously had a slightly weak stomach. After the first show and the first Polish food, we all piled into our ambulance, lights, costumes, etc., Machnic and Kazik at the front and us all in the back, Freddie still feeling a little new. Suddenly there was a small "brrrp" from Freddie's corner, then another, followed by a few more. At first we all politely ignored these noises, obviously coming from Freddie's rear end, but as they continued every few minutes, becoming louder and louder, we started to giggle. Eventually, Eurick said, "Oh! Freddie!" Freddie, looking dreadfully embarrassed, appealed to me, "I can't help it. My tummy is dreadfully upset." The barrage of rude noises grew louder and louder and was almost non-stop. Although we felt sorry, by the time we arrived at our destination we were all pretty well hysterical, and poor Freddie was exhausted by his continuous eruptions. When we arrived the men immediately took charge of him, putting him to bed. It was difficult as we also had a slight language barrier, but later Kazik explained in part sign and Polish that it had been unnecessary to explain Freddie's ailment to the doctor. He just placed the expert at the foot of Freddie's bed where the doctor understood the problem immediately. Sadly from that day Eurick nicknamed my partner Farting Freddie; but he still became a well-liked and hardworking member of our small company.

One dance we performed was really exciting. We learnt the pas de deux called "Pas de Ruban" from Nijinsky's niece. He had danced it with many famous partners. (I made my costume on an old treadle machine.)

While I'm on the seedy part of our tour I might as well tell you about Loda. One night on our tour we arrived rather late. The light in our hut was rather dim but we could hear Loda grumbling from her camp bed that as usual she wanted a pee-pee. Later from her happy muttering we gathered she had found a container, the only trouble being the next morning she found it was a colander! Later when she left with her fiancé, we found an enormous potty and managed to pack it in their suitcase!

The Pas de Ruban

I liked Kazik and continually pestered him. To do him justice I think he thought there was no future for us as his brother was trying to get him to America, so he did try to keep me at a distance, but he always made a fuss, making sure that I was treated extremely well—so well, in fact, the others used to make a joke of it. Eventually I travelled at the front of the ambulance, keeping him awake on the terrible long journeys. One day I noticed a sign "low bridge," which I tried to point out, but he did not understand and smiling at me, said, "Yes, yes!" and drove full speed under the bridge, taking the whole roof off. We were too horrified to look behind us. Amazingly no one was hurt but we had to replace our van.

Machnic made me return inside and Loda was given the privilege of travelling at the front, which turned out to be an almost fatal mistake. Loda, being rather selfish, on the long journeys (of which there were many) just made herself comfortable and went to sleep.

On our way from Derby, with nobody to keep him awake, Kazik fell asleep and crashed at full speed into the back of a horse-drawn muck cart. The horse was killed immediately, but we had only slight injuries. My partner (this was before Freddie) Jan had a dislocated collarbone, and everyone was very shocked, particularly Kazik. Within minutes we were surrounded by helpers and police. I actually finished up on the roof in a field with just a scratch on my hand. The police questioned me, but were most understanding and kind, looking after us. I think we were all in a state of shock.

Eventually we all got to the station and on and off the train at Euston without any money. We found a porter who after hearing our plight lent us all enough money to get a tube home. Later, gladly, I learnt that Machnic had more than reimbursed the porter for his extraordinary kindness. Kazik had to go to court but he was dealt with much understanding, and told he could continue driving on condition that he was not allowed to get so tired. We had to pay for the farmer's horse, for which I believe again Machnic gave more than was demanded.

But the tale does not end there. We had a show to do the

following week and were minus two dancers and one singer. Loda and Yadza said they were too shocked and needed a rest, and Jan of course was out of action. Poor Machnic. After quickly buying a new van, he said if we did not put on the show we would be finished! So Eurick and I had to dance for four. Meesha, Kazik and Machnic did extra numbers. I got to do the Apache Dance, and of course everything had to be learnt within a few hours. It all went most successfully, except Eurick got overexcited and worried when he swung me around by my arm and leg. At the end he was supposed to knock me out, which he did literally, so to Machnic and Kazik's surprise when the curtain parted for our bow I was still unconscious! I recovered rather dazedly for the finale.

Later Machnic was so grateful we celebrated with a drink, which I drank with difficulty, as I had a very swollen and painful jaw, and my chatter was restrained. Poor Kazik had given in to my attentions, and now protected and guarded me almost too much and was far too unforgiving to Eurick for knocking me out. When he found us practising lifts and I had just happened to slip, possibly Eurick had caught me in an odd position, but from that day Kazik never spoke to him. I of course continued to be his friend until he died.

One time Mummy and Daddy came to see the show. I tried to explain that my parents were a little odd, using the Polish word "guppi" (means potty). Kazik immediately put me in my place as the Poles treat their parents with considerable respect. He was dreadfully shocked; in fact, he was so shocked I felt a barrier come between us, but later when they left Kazik apologised, and, though puzzled, he said he had to agree, and yet he liked them! Later he came to stay with us at Heald Green. My parents had returned to almost the same house; it still backed onto what used to be the tennis court, but now was our extended garden.

Mummy decided rather late to give me a few words of advice on the facts of life. These pearls of wisdom were always most amusing. Kazik brought us all tea in bed. My mother said, "I know why I don't like him, he's just like your father!" The latter part of this statement was true but the first part not. She and my father got on extremely well. I think they had one of the most important ingredients in a marriage: conversation, and it never flagged. My father told me, "Better to have someone to row with than no one," something I'm learning the hard way. Maureen and Rowland certainly have this ingredient.

Daddy and I got on so well and I often would relate some of Mummy's words of wisdom to him, such as, "If I had let your father be intimate before we married, he would never have married me." To this revelation we would both roar with laughter. Of course he spoilt her rotten. He did ask me to care for her if anything happened to him, as another saying was, "If I left her she would be like a bull in a china shop; though she is most talented, she has the brain the size of a pigeon's egg."

Mind you he could be naughty. When asked in the village, "How's Mrs Thomas?" he often replied, "Well, thank you, but drinking heavily." Mummy knew of his jokes but never took any notice. Long before Maureen and I arrived, and then probably short of money, Daddy out of the blue bought her a large new car, which he drove from Manchester even though he was extremely short-sighted, slightly deaf and had never driven before. Quite a feat! He arranged then for someone to teach Mummy to drive. He himself never drove again.

While I'm on the subject of marriage, one small word of advice to my family. I long for them to be continually happy, but if there is the slightest problem, don't hide it or it will grow into an incurable barrier.

The car

Life with this small Polish company was fun. When Christmas arrived I, as usual, took the turkey or goose home. On one occasion when I nearly missed the train home, Kazik pushed me onto the moving train and under the amazed gaze of the passengers in the carriage my goose was thrown in after me. This was the time when we were performing at a forestry camp. They treated their trees like gold, but gave me permission to have a fir tree on the condition I chose and cut down my own. This was lovely. Some of the others and I went to try and find the smallest tree possible, and there it was, looking so tiny and perfect amongst the giants. Eurick tied it up as tight as possible, but when it was on its own we found it was enormous. We put it on the train, Daddy picked it up and with a great deal of hassle, according to him, got it on the bus.

3

Eventually when I was about twenty-four I decided to retire. I cannot explain my attitude to life at that time; I just seemed to plunge on without thinking of the future, almost as if it was all planned. Granny Alderley tried hard to advise me, but I plodded on regardless. I hired halls, taught, gave shows and started preparations to marry Kazik. All I could think of was that he would play the piano wonderfully, we would find premises, start a school, and life would settle into normality. But there was one problem: we had no money.

On one of those weekends home from a show I called at the old school to see how the two girls were getting on. It was well-known and thriving, but on arrival I found that only one girl was in charge, the other having left. While I sat and had coffee, to my horror all was revealed! She spoke quite openly to me as if I had known all along: "As you know we lived as man and wife, but when you left I fell in love with Mrs A (I'm not mentioning any names; she was the pianist who had a young daughter), but then I had an affair with B, one of our pupils (I knew the girl; she must have been very young at the time)." I couldn't get out of the place quick enough. Of all my experiences this sickened me the most. How many children (myself nearly) had been influenced?

Mrs Ben Moston lived only a few minutes away. I almost collapsed at her home. How wonderful she was, giving me tea, listening to my story, and understanding immediately. I was in a state of shock but she soon brought me back to reality. She was such a clever and lovely woman. Strangely she wrote a poem about that very visit which was printed in *Punch* on January 4, 1950. The beginning lines go thus: "When Meeta comes to tea she moves into the room like cherry bloom." There's a whole page of flattering poetry with not a word of the horrible situation I had left.

It was not long after this that I saw it: Fellowship House for sale. It was only a few doors away from Miss Richardson's private school, where I had received my only two years of education.

I wanted the place immediately. It was perfect. I was friendly with a Mr and Mrs Peers, and I taught nearly all their six beautiful and talented offspring. Mr Peers had a good speaking voice and was a prominent member of the Northenden Players, the very ones that Mummy, Daddy, Aunty Peggy, Uncle Tom Cobbly and all had been members of years before. He often helped me with announcements in my shows; in fact, he and his wife were a great help. Unfortunately Mr. Peers had a dreadful fault: women, all of us! We (women) dared never be left alone with him. On these occasions he was rather like Les Dawson's version of the lecherous man or worse, only good-looking. Some women even liked it. What I could never understand was that when I appealed to Mrs Peers she just laughed. Many years later Mr Peers' daughter brought him to see me at my cottage when he was 90. I was so pleased to see him but his outrageous behaviour was no different.

Fellowship House on right

The Players had thought of buying Fellowship House, as it was bigger than their premises near the river in Boat Lane, but the price of £4,000 was too much. Mr Peers got them to give me all the information on it, including quite an expensive survey that they had paid for. When Granny Alderley realised I was interested in the place her behaviour was quite strange. She spoke of it in hushed and disgusted tones, "A workman's club! If you do buy it you have to change its name," but I was just like Toad of Toad Hall: I had fallen in love with it; I wanted it and its name. I'm afraid Kazik was in the same category, poor man! I got in touch with Stockport Mersey Building Society, as one of my pupil's fathers suggested they might help me. I can see them now, three old gentlemen from the firm pretending to dance in the large room at Fellowship House, and agreeing that it was the perfect place for me.

It had a fairly imposing appearance. What had been the billiard and conference room was quite large, with a huge fireplace, a cloakroom, and toilet with an entrance. This part was in good order and was separated by a long corridor from a tall two-storied part, which I thought would be our living accommodation. This was almost derelict; there was a terrible smell of damp rot, which was rampant. All the wood was covered with mushrooms as big as saucers. The room at the front's floor was wood that was soft like chewing gum. The middle room had a large black iron range, possibly six feet high and seven feet wide, with ovens and hooks for goodness-knows-what. The back room was a sort of kitchen with a low, brown, shallow sink with a cold water tap that swung loose at the end of a lead pipe. There was a cooker but only the grill worked, and one had to turn and hold it if one wanted to cook something on top. These rooms had floors of reject gravestones, some with the names and dates still on them. "Caroline" was carved on one.

Upstairs there were two rooms but no bathroom or toilet. At the back was an outside toilet, a yard, and a very small garden the length of the building. The back door was rotten, but the door to the studio (as I called it) and the front door into the corridor dividing the building were most imposing, like church doors, large, arched tops, heavy oak with large ornate black hinges and door knockers. The date was on the front, dating back about one hundred years.

I received a letter from Mersey Building Society offering me a mortgage of £800, so I rang the agents and offered them £750. That conversation must have been amusing. They were quite short with me, saying that they couldn't suggest such an offer to their client. My answer was, "But that's all I've got, and I want it."

While this was going on I decided to try and make a bit of extra money, so I danced in the chorus in a pantomime under a different name. All professionals say everyone ought to do at least one panto, it's such fun, and it's absolutely true. My panto was in Salford, *Jack and the Beanstalk*.

Sandy Powell was a marvellous Dame, one of the best. In a particular scene he wore a knitted frock down to his ankles. It had large bands of bright colours and was very tight (his wife, who was Jack, I believe, had knitted it). What with his rather portly body, over-padded bosom, very manly voice and the thick glasses (he was extremely short-sighted), the jokes were scarcely heard for the laughter.

Then there was the giant. When he first boomed, "Fee fie foe fum," through the amplifier I was caught completely by surprise, and experienced the fear I had had at Holly Bank at the age of three on our small stage. I danced with a group of six girls. One of our numbers was similar to the Tiller girls, a tap dance (something I had never done on stage). We dressed as guards at Buckingham Palace, all red and black and extremely smart, except I always seemed to pick up the only mangy Busby. The other number was a rather glamorous moonlight scene, when we wore long, dark blue chiffon gowns and carried branches with fairy lights that we switched on—most effective, except there again mine frequently didn't light!

It was getting nearer to my wedding day, and there was still no word about Fellowship House. I had made my wedding dress, a luscious cream satin Jacques Fath pattern, most successful I thought. Sheila Paxton and Vera Dawson were to be my ladies-in-waiting. Kazik, who was staying at the time at one of my pupil's homes, had got one of his Polish friends to be his best man. One morning the phone rang. It was the agent to say Mrs Smith had amazingly accepted my offer of £750. Then my solicitor agreed (although he said it was not the correct procedure) to send me the key immediately, as we only had a few weeks to go.

Kazik and Daddy were the first to go in one night. It seems there was no need for the key, as the back door fell in. Then Kazik fainted. Daddy said it was the terrible smell of dry rot; in fact, Kazik said that was the reason, but I think it was shock. Poor man! He put up with an awful lot, but strangely he never complained. The next day everybody went into action. Mr and Mrs Peers and many of my pupils' parents all set to work. It was intended that the guests would go immediately into the dance hall and never see down the hallway into the living quarters, which Daddy and others had compared to the chamber of horrors. Only the helpers were allowed in the back.

The hall was transformed, firstly by a decorator whom I didn't even know! He decorated the room in one afternoon, as a wedding present he said. He used "Pongo magnolia," and he left me a gallon of the paint, saying, "It might come in useful," which it certainly did; I Pongoed everywhere later.

Sheila and Vera did all the flowers, decorating the hall beautifully. The trestle tables were laden with food. Daddy's lifelong friend Wilf Webster (Butterball) was in charge of a well-stocked bar, his contribution. Centre stage of course was Mummy's elegantly decorated wedding cake. As I said she could do anything.

We were to be married at St Chad's Catholic Church. The young priest was quite upset, as it seems according to their rules a mixed marriage was not entitled to flowers or music. St Chad's was not an attractive church, but rather plain and foreboding, not like the beautiful old church at the top of Boat Lane, so altogether it looked as if the ceremony was going to be a rather dismal occasion.

When the great day arrived I got up early, only to be sent straight back to bed by my grandmother, saying, "No bride gets up for breakfast." She brought a tray with a boiled egg, dippies, tea, a flower, and a letter from the solicitor (which I have to this day) wishing me all the best and with a cheque for thirty pounds, the change. Later he told me he had never experienced such an odd arrangement.

Eventually, about eleven, everyone had left for the church and my father and I were alone waiting for Mr Pollitt, the taxi man (also one of the parents). We had a short rehearsal, but we were both so nervous we couldn't think which side to walk on, until Daddy suddenly remembered. When we got in the taxi Daddy sat at the front and I sat in the back. What could go wrong? There were some beautiful small silver flower arrangements inside the cab, I remember lily of the valley. My mother had watered them. As we got to the top of Stepping Hill the taxi jolted, I bounced up, the containers emptied onto my seat, and I sat back in a pool of water. I cried for them to stop. Jumping out, I turned my back on my surprised father, saying, "What does it look like?" Daddy's answer: "Just like a map of Australia."

While still clutching my bouquet of peace roses, I ran up the path of a magnificent white bungalow, strangely one I had often wondered what its interior was like. The door was opened by a portly, distinguished gentleman. I turned, showing my wet bottom and saying, "Look what's happened! Can you help me, please?"

Heaven knows what he thought at first but he didn't hesitate, and while explaining that all the servants and his wife were out, he found an iron and board, which he placed in the large front room, and drew the curtains by remote control. I was impressed. He then had to undo the long zip down my back and discreetly stayed behind the door within hearing ("In case you need me," he said). There I was ironing my dress in nothing but bra, pants, stockings, suspenders, high heels and a borrowed blue garter, all the time grumbling, "If it doesn't come out I'm not going!" It did; being only water it was perfect. Mr Booth (who I found out later was the owner of many cake shops) zipped me up and approved. Weeks later my mother was playing Bridge when her partner Mrs Booth said, "The strangest thing happened to my husband...."

I arrived at the church about twenty minutes late. There were flowers up the aisle and on the altar, and a Polish choir sang loudly up in the gallery. Mrs Ben Moston remarked that when they first sang they gave her a shock, they were so loud and unexpected. Heaven knows how the priest allowed it, but from then on everyone was happy. Speeches at lunch were abundant. Daddy, I believe, was at his best. Kazik, sadly, was so nervous he read the speech, but later when we were on honeymoon (Maureen and Rowland lent us their tiny but pretty cottage at Longridge) Kazik showed me how he could give his speech without his notes. We only spent one night there. The rest we spent in, of all places, Blackpool, probably because it was cheap.

We rang up Fellowship House very late on the day of our wedding, knowing that Daddy was to spend the night there as it was not possible to lock the place. We were surprised to hear that the party was still going on and everyone was really enjoying themselves. One man got rather drunk and went into the forbidden land across the hallway. He went through the rotten floor up to his thighs and was rescued with great difficulty. Mrs Grout also got slightly giddy, and to my mother's annoyance spilt her champagne all over the saved cake crumbs.

And so married life began. It was fun. We decided to sleep in the back room upstairs. Our friends had tried their best in between getting the hall ready, so in the bedroom they had put a kettle on a long, flexible gas pipe, a bowl, etc., and arranged a sort of thing to hang our clothes on, which collapsed straightaway. Kazik, wanting to please me (this he did all the time), arranged a tin bath in the back kitchen with a screen around it. After filling it with water he triumphantly called me, but when I went to step in I found all the water had seeped away through a hole and through the gravestones. We were so busy, working like beavers. We pulled out every bit of rotten wood and burnt the bricks (which were handmade) with a blow lamp; the mortar had horse hair I think…or would it be cow's?

Kazik had a terrible job at Frederick Smith's Wire Company, where he was working outside winding wire and stacking it. I felt dreadfully guilty as I had got him the work through my cousin on my father's side. (I never thought he did us any favours.) Kazik would come home stinking of copper, and to add to the insult, they, knowing he was a concert pianist, expected him to play for their choir free, which being Kazik he did. But it was not long before he was in charge of the store, still smelly but inside and making more money.

He would come home and go straight to the piano to play for my classes. Sometimes I had to keep him from falling asleep. I would see him leaning to the right and would give him a nudge. I took a course in modelling at Lucy Clayton's and did some extra work modelling in the mornings at a wholesalers in Manchester. I taught dancing after school; Saturday mornings were our busiest. I also took two keep fit classes after eight p.m. There was a rather nice large wooden sign in a Gothic style outside the hall's entrance, which I painted black and put the wording in gold: "Northenden Ballet School."

One day Kazik decided to remove the iron range, as Uncle Ted had given us as a wedding present a beautiful brick fireplace. Daddy and I stayed in the kitchen with a blanket over the door. Daddy always stayed with us while Mummy played Bridge, but he set to and helped. There was a lot of banging and Polish utterances, then suddenly an ominous silence. Daddy and I knew instinctively that something was wrong, and we held our breath! Then there was a dreadful crash. We expected to see Kazik looking like a gingerbread man, squashed. The range must have missed him by only a few inches. He was flat against the wall, his face white. The range had fallen, covering the whole floor. Kazik said, "I just couldn't hold it!"

The years passed very quickly, and we decided to make our lounge larger by knocking into the hallway. While Kazik was at work I decided to surprise him and start on it. I was amazed how easy it was, and had soon knocked a large hole and had a pile of bricks, when there was a knock at the door. I answered it, and without saying a word the man (whom I did not know) raced past me and immediately built a column up. "I was going to surprise my husband," I said. "You certainly would, madam, I think that's the main wall." Sadly we had to pay builders to fix a steel girder but it was great when done.

The next step was central heating. Kazik gradually brought from work all the pipes and radiators, and between us—me the workman's mate and Kazik the brains—we installed heating and hot water and a separate bathroom at the end of our bedroom. Actually I had mentioned I would like a sunken bath; this Kazik started but sadly never finished. I even forgot why we stepped up on bare wooden boards that were placed around the bath! But we were proud of our house. The back door, the one Daddy and Kazik had kicked down, was now a French window opening out onto a patio with pond lights and fountain!

We were often approached by people who wanted to hire our hall for jumble sales, etc., but even though we were short of money we hated the idea, as it felt as if our home was being invaded. When a certain lady (a medium) who lived opposite approached us, we accepted happily! We didn't mind her hiring our room, which she did for years until I left. The spiritualists entered at the side door and we never heard a sound! Madame Acarti was about fifty, large, and had a beard! According to her, on their first meeting the reception was wonderful! She was extremely happy. Kazik often said to me he wished we had a spy hole just to see what was going on!

I did actually let the room without letting Kazik know. I wanted to buy him a drill and a fob watch, so as I was approached by a carpet salesman and the money was marvellous, I went into business. But it led to problems. Kazik left for work at eight and the carpet man arrived at eight thirty, so there were some hair-raising and embarrassing moments. Sometimes the man would come too soon when Kazik had only just left. I would drag the carpet man in by his lapels, saying, "My husband hasn't turned the corner yet." With my usual luck the carpet man seemed to understand and entered into the spirit. The funniest time was when Kazik returned home and wondered what the smell was in the hall.

My dear cousin Martin Thomas (Daddy's brother's son, then seventeen, the only one of his family I really liked who used to come and stay with us when on holiday as his parents lived in Egypt) was horrified when the carpet man came and insisted on lending me the money I needed. I accepted but continued my liaison with my carpet man. He was actually of gypsy descent. I think the family were originally from the fair.

I found that I had ties to Fellowship House from way back. Firstly I was approached outside by the Great Aunt Jess, who was then in her nineties. She addressed me as Miss Polly, and then explained, "I know you're not her, she died of a broken heart when only twenty-five, but you do so resemble her." After this I made enquiries and found out that the infamous Major Jock Hillkirk had given penny readings in my hall. Gentleman would sometimes read the Bible or excerpts from literature, which the illiterate would pay a penny for, and Aunt Polly (my great aunt) would play the organ. As I investigated further I found that my birth had also been registered in my new home when the local council used it. This only made me love the place more. I would walk through the hall in the dark; it held no fears for me, even straight after Madame in her gold lamé had held a lengthy séance. I never saw any ghosts. Mind you I did sometimes hear the piano in the hall tinkle, but put this down to the change of atmosphere.

Time passed quickly. When I was nearly thirty Kazik asked if I wanted a family. He said it was up to me. My decision (of course) was we had to; it was the normal thing to do and our house was fit for a baby!

By this time Mummy and Daddy had moved into a cottage in Kenworthy Lane only five minutes walk from us, and they spent far too much time with us. Daddy and Kazik got on extremely well, which was odd really because they were very much alike, except perhaps Daddy had a rather more mischievous humour. But Kazik and Mummy, that was quite different; they did and yet they didn't. The strangest thing of all was when Kazik learnt one Friday that his accordionist was ill; in fact he'd died. Kazik had formed a small dance band who played most Saturdays at the Polish Club, Cheetham Hill; their music consisted mostly of Polish Mazurkas and ordinary popular music. Kazik was in a state, as the accordion is an essential part of Polish music, so I suggested he phone my mother. The next evening off she went all dressed up and looking beautiful. Kate played the piano while Kazik played the accordion.

From that day on she became a fully-fledged member. She told me, "Kazik picks up his accordion and stamps his foot while calling 'One, two, three, go!' and all my music falls on the floor." Another story was, "Every time a man flatters me, Kazik says he's either drunk or mad!"

During these musical sessions Daddy and I kept each other company. I had now become pregnant, was taking no alcohol and was thinking beautiful thoughts! I wanted a beautiful blonde boy! Not much hope, as both Kazik and I were very dark. I stopped weighing myself when I was fifteen stone; my normal weight was nine. Kazik would help me into the dancing room; I would arrange my frock around my huge tum and then call the pupils in.

Marek arrived at just the right time: October 22, mid-term holidays, so work wasn't held up. The first part of the fortuneteller in Egypt came true. As Marek arrived, the nurse exclaimed, "Red hair!" but this changed almost immediately and I got my really beautiful flaxen-haired child almost identical to the child in my baby book! Kazik and I were over the moon. He was so lovely and yet as he grew so very funny, running around in his tiny Wellies talking to himself.

One day at the age of about three he brushed outside and managed to break three windows. His charm was his willingness to try and help me, especially when I determined that he should have a friend and I became pregnant again.

This baby, a little girl, I lost. She was nine pounds. I named her Anna Maureen. There was just enough room for her small coffin to be buried with Granny and Grandpa Alderley and Grandpa's parents.

Except for this sad episode things were progressing well. I did some choreography for The Didsbury Operatic. Although they were amateurs they paid me a reasonable amount. On one occasion we did *Song of Norway*. It made me so happy as I got

Kazik to take part. They supplied him with a grand piano and he played the Grieg Concerto quite brilliantly, and was made a great fuss of.

About this time things in Poland were a little easier and Kazik visited his father. Then his father, Grandpa Poland (as we called him), came to England, also his brother came from America. He was now in his forties but they hadn't seen him since his father had sent him on a ship to America at the age of seventeen!

I fell pregnant again and I was sick and huge as usual. I couldn't sleep on my back or my side until Kazik hit on the idea of putting a pillow under my tum, then I got cramp and what with laughing, screaming and being quite unable to move, I had Kazik terribly upset, vowing never to go through it again!

Stephen arrived, once again well-timed—August 30, during holidays—and again the fortuneteller's words came true, as he appeared with red hair, which thankfully turned brown. According to my fortune I had to lose one more child and marry again!

My mother brought me home but amazingly left me on the doorstep with Marek with the words, "I must dash to Bridge." With difficulty I managed to get to bed with Stephen in a carrycot. Marek, aged four, said, "How can I help, Mummy?" My heartless reply was "Go away as far and as quietly as possible," which he did, and I rested until he appeared, most upset and saying, "I went so far away I couldn't get back in time." Bending over, he showed me a rather dirty and smelly bottom, as he was only four. But we managed. Life could be fun!

I always had a lady help. When I think about this I suppose it was a bit odd, but I did, and got on well with all, particularly Kitty Pomfret, who stayed with me for about thirty years. We're still friends; I believe she is ninety. As I miss her, I've called my cat Kitty. We do occasionally chat over the phone.

When Kazik's father came to stay, Grandpa Poland and Daddy went off together one morning. We were all curious how the two men got on, as although my father could speak a few languages it didn't cover German or Polish. I was delighted when they came home very late, having obviously had a great time. Daddy had taken Grandpa P. to the Royal Cotton Exchange and also to his many Manchester haunts.

We were very lucky with babysitters. An Irish family had two nice girls, student nurses, Philomena and Carmel; also our friends Kath and Norman Worrill were happy to borrow our babies, especially on Saturdays, and of course Daddy was always willing. Sadly he died (just after he had told them both one of his stories about a character he called Jimson) when Marek was about seven and Stephen three.

So life continued. Stephen one morning came down from their room and said, "Marek wants to know what you would give him if he passed to Manchester Grammar?" Daft as usual I said, "Anything." Stephen replied, "Well, will you give me a tape measure? We want to measure the bedroom for an elephant."

I think Kazik was a very happy man. He would say, "If I died tomorrow I die happy, but I wouldn't like to leave you as you would never manage on your own," an odd thing to say as little did we know that I would be managing on my own for over thirty years.

Yes, things were going reasonably smoothly except for one small thing: I was not happy! Difficult to explain. One would say I was getting all I had worked for: interesting home, lovely boys, kind, interesting and doting husband. I just could not cope. My grandma said, "Once you've made your bed you must sleep in it." I was at first happy to do this. I loved Kazik, but after twenty years of turning into my usual dead duck every time poor Kazik made love (which was frequently), it became wearing to pretend, especially after a day of the nursery, some private lessons, and then a keep fit class. I was in no mood to do my great act, however fond I was of him. Still I carried on, but it does have, as everything does, its amusing side.

In desperation I asked my good friend Kathy Worrill, who was a registered nurse, for advice. She told me as I didn't want to upset him, get the boys to bed early, put my most glamorous outfit on and get it over early, which would enable me to get to sleep before midnight, something I desperately believed in. Well, Kathy phoned later in the week to hear how her advice had gone. Very successful! Kazik was thrilled! But he expected the same at midnight. Kathy and I often had a laugh.

When Stephen was about one year old, Kathy burst into tears, saying she and Norman had been married over ten years and still had no family. I cheered her up by jokingly saying, "Leave it to me!" I had seen these natives do a fertility dance holding flowers. The only flowers Kathy could find were plastic, which I remarked might have unusual results. I placed Stephen in the middle of Kathy and Norman's bed and to the astonished little Stephen and Kathy's laughter, I pranced very seriously around and over. Two weeks later Kathy missed her period and had two children. I know it's rubbish but perhaps it made her relax when she lay in bed with Norman and visualized my crazy antics. Whatever it was it did the trick. So except for my problem things couldn't be better. We were really proud of what we had achieved, and increasing Kazik's happiness, Marek got to Manchester Grammar, all free, and seemingly quite easily.

To top all this, one day Kazik asked me what I thought of him accepting quite a responsible job, still with Frederick Smiths, but an office job, white collar—and this was the worrying part: two telephones to answer. He felt his English was not quite up to this task. My answer was, "Don't do it if it's going to upset you." His answer: "I've already done it for a week!"

Kazik took a holiday for one day. We spent such an enjoyable time in Stockport, as we didn't get much time to ourselves. We ended up buying, instead of the much-needed washing machine, a record player with two amplifiers. It was well worth it, as we had some lovely records, classical of course, but the Beatles too. Coming back we clambered to the top of the bus. When it was nearly at our stop I was unable to awake Kazik. I realised he was not in a natural sleep but he did eventually come around. I knew there was something wrong, but he did not even remember so I was unable to get him to understand he must see a doctor, although he did promise to see the nurse at work.

As he now had a better job we bought a rather funny small secondhand blue van, I suppose suitable for his band. It was about this time I decided it would be easier for me to teach and enter my pupils for the the Royal Academy of Dancing Exams, but to do this they wanted me to pay all my back subscription, which I hadn't paid since I was eighteen! So although I hadn't danced for twenty years I decided to go back to my original teacher in Deansgate Manchester, Miss Muriel Tweedy. According to the students the senior exams were quite difficult to get, but I attended classes, sometimes taking a very young Stephen, who would stare wide-eyed as his mother would cavort on point. I got my Elementary then my Intermediate with very little problem and was ready to take my Advanced; in fact another student and I demonstrated in white tutus, pink tights, and points at an RAD lecture!

But then disaster: I found I was pregnant! I was forty-seven. I got someone to help my partner Joan Tucker with the nursery and off I went for a consultation with a well-known specialist who had originated from Miss Richardson's private school. I was so nervous and for some reason didn't want him to know me, but thought there was no possibility as my name was Piatkowski. He was most understanding but suggested as I had no help (my mother didn't want to know), at my age and considering I wanted to continue working, the only solution was an abortion.

I was horrendously upset. I didn't tell the boys, but when I suggested them having a brother or sister they were not impressed with the idea. Things from then on moved extremely fast. The specialist, it seemed, did recognise me and was obviously moved by my tears and predicament. I found myself in a private room at the hospital, everything free. But it wasn't that simple. I was found to be too far gone for a normal abortion. I ended up having quite an operation, a caesarean. It was all horrible. They had difficulty in getting me to sign for it to be done. It was only when I was so drugged that I succumbed.

When I'd visited the specialist the first time I was in such a state I left my knickers in his office! As I said before, even the worst situations have an amusing side. There was a girl who was having problems conceiving in the hospital. She was slightly simple, and when I came around from the anaesthetic she was standing at the foot of my bed and reassured me with the words, "Don't worry, I'm sure you'll have another."

The two Irish nurses were really quite unkind to me although I was in considerable pain, but strangely later they both came and said they were very sorry. It seems they thought I was a lot younger. From then on they were most friendly, telling me that the simple girl who couldn't conceive, after an examination the doctors found she was a virgin. She and her husband had slept for twelve years with their pet dog between them, not knowing what to do. So you see, although there were tears there was laughter as well.

Miss Tweedie, when she found out I was pregnant, sat very erect and in her most dictatorial and haughty manner said, "I can cope with a forty-seven-year-old woman in my class, but no way can I teach a forty-seven-year-old pregnant one. For heaven's sake go and sort yourself out!" For all her stern exterior, I think she quite liked me. She sent us some really unusual cocktail glasses as a wedding present, and later when my problems got worse she was very kind.

While I was going through these traumas I managed to get a friend, Gerald Spicer, to take my classes for me. We managed to take a few weeks holiday on a boat on the Thames. Mummy came and helped with the cost. We had a luxury boat. Kate was installed in a large cabin with a separate bathroom; the boys and Simon, Marek's friend, had bunk beds in another cabin. Kazik and I were in the galley on a put-u-up. There was also a second bathroom. We had a good holiday. At the beginning the doctor had supplied me with tranquillisers, which I counted feverishly, worried least I ran out. I didn't realise how vulnerable I was, but the taking of the pills with rum and Coke was soon forgotten, and I only remembered the rum. I can see Kazik now, being ordered about by my mother, arranging a mattress on deck so she could sunbathe in comfort.

One day in a lock some young men asked me out for a drink. They said something about my mother and father. It was then I realised how old Kazik was looking. Sometimes we would try and escape to the pub for a drink as we got very little time on our own, but Mummy was quite annoyed that we wanted her to stay on board. Actually now I'm writing it down, the boys were old enough to be left—Marek and Simon were nearly sixteen and Stephen twelve—but we just wanted to have a little time away. She still managed to make me feel guilty.

When we got back home, it was business as usual. Winter was approaching. Kazik and Mummy were busy with the band. Kazik had quite a bad cold but carried on. Christmas Eve we were both up terribly late making a frame for Mummy's Christmas present, a picture we knew she wanted. By two a.m. we were still struggling with it, me holding it together while Kazik pinned and glued. Kazik's words were, "Your mother will be the death of me!"

New Year's Eve came, and as usual that night Kazik put his arms around me, and for the first time I refused. I turned my back on him and cried silently, knowing how hurtful I was being, but I just couldn't cope.

New Year's Day I awoke, slipped quietly out of bed and went to the butcher's next door to collect the goose. When I returned, Marek, white-faced, met me, saying, "Don't go upstairs, Mummy!" It seems that poor Marek and his friend Rick had lifted Kazik onto the bed. He had died in an instant!

4

I can't explain how I felt. It was as if I was standing on the edge of a precipice, I couldn't get my breath, I couldn't eat, everything tasted like cotton wool. I rang my sister straightaway and quite unbelievably she and Rowland appeared like magic! I don't think they were any longer than a few hours and yet it was at least six-hour journey. I missed him dreadfully, and yet I'd wished him gone! It didn't make sense. In fact nothing made sense for many years. With it being Christmas I was able to see to the funeral and arrange for a pianist, Mrs Jones (nice, kind, helpful woman) to play for me.

I stopped the nursery and took a job in the mornings at an old folks' home; that in itself is worth writing about. All the people, workers and inmates, were interesting, but I have only time for one anecdote. Annie, a resident, had been a prostitute and even in her nineties one could see she had been a rather pretty blonde, and what a character. We had an excellent matron, and one evening it was a special party night with everyone enjoying themselves. I went to speak to Annie, who seemed to have dozed off with her gin and tonic at her side and a red rose in her hair. I asked the matron should I wake her, and the Matron said, "Good heavens, no! She's dead but she wouldn't like to miss her last party."

About three weeks after Kazik died, the phone rang one night. It seems my mother had fallen outside her Bridge club and had not only broken her hip but also her femur. I could hear her screams, which was unusual as she was a brave woman. She was lucky in one way, as her partner was a surgeon and attended to her immediately. Joan Tucker (such a good friend) gave me a lift to the hospital. Thankfully my mother was reasonably comfortable, but as always situations have their comical side. I took my large bottle of Chanel that Kazik had given me and as I dabbed my mother's forehead with it she gasped, "That's lovely, where did you get it?" When I mentioned Kazik she burst into tears, saying, "What am I going to do without him?"

She had never stopped being rude about him. I'm afraid I couldn't help finding it funny, even though my situation was obviously getting worse by the minute.

To try and cheer her up I spent some of my hard-earned money on two rather special nighties, which later I found she had got the nurses to cut off up to the waist as she said they were uncomfortable. My nightmare continued to get worse as my mother needed looking after for a few months. As she could only walk with great difficulty, I put a bed in our living room and a commode under the stairs!

I was in a sort of daze, but there is no excuse for my behaviour from then on. All I can say is I wish I could go back and relive those dreadful days, if only to put right all the mistakes I made, the worst being I never stopped to think how lucky I was. I had two boys helping me when they desperately needed help themselves; they, in fact, behaved and coped better than I. They finished Manchester Grammar and Stephen got to King's College Cambridge; Marek possibly didn't do as well as he should, which I will always feel was my fault, and sometimes I think he knows this and blames me, which he has every right to. But it's too late; I can only say that I'm sorry.

While Mummy was installed in our main room I escaped in a daze into my bedroom with bottles of gin and martini. One night there was a knock at my bedroom window. It was a quite good-looking young man of twenty-five called Peter, who had previously been to mend the electricity. At the time Mother had probably noticed him looking at me because when he had gone she came out with the statement, "That side of your life (meaning men) is over now and you and I will manage." Maybe that was just the wrong thing to say to me, rather like a red rag to a bull. Anyway, back to Peter, who asked me to go dancing. I don't think I had actually been social dancing more than ten times in the whole of my life, so I accepted.

I loved that sort of dancing. I can only recall a few times when I did. One time was when Ronnie Cliffe asked me when I was thirteen and Mummy dressed me up like a little girl in a frock she made from someone's wedding dress because she said one had to wear white the first time. Ronnie, who was seventeen, was so embarrassed and wanted me to go and change but I obviously couldn't. It was a miserable evening because he felt silly with me with my baby doll dress on. Another time I did manage to go once to the dance hall at Wilmslow, then Mr Moston took me to

Oddininos. Oh! And the Count took me to a dinner dance at the Midland Hotel, but altogether there was very little dancing. And of course it all went from bad to worse. I ended up in Peter's seedy flat and as usual became a dead duck because I realised that if I wanted a cuddle, I couldn't have that without the other, and I was desperately missing the former.

Straight after this I felt rather odd, you know when your fingers go dead; the whole of my right side was affected in this way. I went to the doctor, who asked me if I had had a shock within the last few days. She said it would wear off eventually. But my problems had not ended yet.

Peter gave Joan and Stephen and me a lift to Manchester Grammar's carol service; we never got there. A woman came out of a side road and bashed into us. Luckily I was the only one hurt and taken to hospital. My face had to have quite a lot of stitches in it and it looked so awful I had to wear a veil so as not to upset my pupils.

The next problem: I was called to Manchester Grammar. It seems the boys, after impeccable behaviour at school, were now causing concern. When the master saw me he was quite visibly upset. It seems they should have been told of our misfortunes. He said he hoped it was not too late for them to attempt to help, although a year had already passed since Kazik died.

Things went from bad to worse. My behaviour did not improve. I just did not stop and think. A builder, Ken Fryer, for whom Peter worked, found out I liked lobster, and as he was a deep sea diver in his spare time he appeared at my door with a large live lobster that he later cooked for me. In a way perhaps Ken was a better influence in the following few years. He wasn't a bad-looking man, tall, about thirty-seven, a bachelor, and the most important thing he did try to help, and genuinely seemed to like the boys.

I treated him appallingly. I had just been to see a film with Rowland's sister, *A Touch of Class* starring Glenda Jackson. It was about a woman who on a whim went on an exciting holiday with a complete stranger. Who says the media doesn't affect us? One day while Ken was knee-deep in rotten flooring in the cloakroom, repairing it for nothing, trying to help us, I said, "Take me away." Ken, still quite a stranger, looked surprised. I said, "Take me somewhere far away, somewhere exciting, ANYWHERE!" To my surprise this rather ordinary, humdrum man immediately booked a holiday. From that moment things went even more topsy turvy. Firstly the agent went bankrupt; Ken lost his money. I, being horrible, said, "If you don't arrange something soon I'm not going," so he booked a luxury holiday privately on the island of EIba.

Mummy, who had recovered by this time, took us to the airport. When we arrived there was a horrendous storm, something they said did not usually occur. Because of this the normal ferry was not working, which meant Ken was put to more expense going an awful way around by taxi. Eventually we arrived at a magnificent hotel. We stepped into the lift, which started to behave in a most erratic way, starting and stopping, opening and shutting its doors until I, who didn't like lifts anyway, screamed for Ken to put a stop to it, which he did by quickly putting his foot in the door as it momentarily opened. We finished by walking up four floors.

Our room was magnificent with a large balcony, but when we entered the shower it exploded mud! Eventually we got down to dinner, then all the lights went out. As the staff were not used to such storms, they did not have enough candles, so we ate our meal in the dark.

But things got much worse. I was not due for a period for a few weeks, but I started early with gusto. Before I could do anything the sheet was covered, and Ken fainted! Me: "What on earth are you doing?" Ken: "I'm terribly sorry, I sometimes faint at the sight of blood!" I managed to wrap myself in the sheet but I was so bad I dared not sit up. All the time I had a white-faced Ken quite speechless, his large brown eyes reminding me of a seal. I lay there helpless and explained to Ken that as this was unexpected I was quite unprepared, so he would have to go and buy some extra large sanitary pads. Poor Ken, he was a real mother's boy, but he set off, promising he would return with the necessaries as quickly as he could.

Hours passed until eventually a triumphant but obviously harassed Ken appeared. It seems he could not find any on the island and had gone on the ferry. His escapades in the large stores sounded unbelievable. No one spoke English and the distraught Ken had to resort to mimicry before he actually got what he wanted. The helpful female assistant had brought everything out, from tablecloths and napkins to babies' nappies. Thank goodness he had succeeded. I was able to bring things to a reasonably normal situation, sheets and towels all hung over the balcony!

We did have a marvellous holiday. We saw Napoleon's palace and sat on a floating restaurant having lobster and wine. On the way home we caught a small aircraft, which landed in Pisa so I could see the leaning tower. Ken did his very best to please; at least I think he enjoyed my company and thought it was worth it, although maybe he was a little puzzled sometimes.

It was about this time that Tom Powell, Rowland's brother-in-law, called. He was an extremely intellectual man; he and my father both worked in cotton. He had no time for fools, and was not an easy man if you didn't happen to be on his level of conversation. He said he was going on an annual visit to someone. He thought it would interest me, and to come at once! Off we went, me full of curiosity, and Tom with a bottle of vintage whisky. We arrived at a picturesque but dilapidated cottage and stepped into a small room where there were at least three comely ladies bustling about with their hats on (that I noticed particularly). There, lying propped up on spotless white pillows in a large bed, was Tom Power, still as handsome as ever, the gorgeous thick, curly hair with just a sprinkling of grey, his face lined and weather-beaten. He took the whiskey and then, looking past Tom Powell, recognition came into those twinkling eyes. "Come me, darlin', you're old enough for a kiss now. 'Tis beautiful you are." He held out his arms. I had waited forty years for that kiss!

I was puzzled how these two such different men had become friends. It seems that when the fair came to the croft and Tom was doing his usual job as resident boxer, Tom Powell had challenged him to a fight and won! And they had been friends ever since. What a strange friendship! The Oxford man and the uneducated rogue—obviously not only women were captivated by his charm. Tom Power died about a week later, over eighty.

After this we visited the Heald Green Hotel. Tom Powell was obviously taking me down memory lane. The hotel was a place of many memories before and during the war. Daddy went for his regular pint escorted by the cat Peestole, who would walk at his side through the gardens and wait to escort him home. Daddy would meet Tom and a few others. The Civil Defence also met there. This was where I wore that dreadful white dress for my first dance with Ronnie, where Maureen had her twenty-first party and we ate all Grandpa's marvellous asparagus and strawberries, not forgetting my ballroom classes at the age of fifteen when Tom Powell and also many young men from the armed forces attended, learning slow, slow, quick, quick, slow.

As Tom and I sat sipping our drinks and reminiscing, he suddenly came out with a most incongruous confession. He actually said he had been jealous of Kazik, and now I was free, if

I would marry him he would leave Kath; I was taken aback but realised that Kath and he were inseparable, always would be, BUT they both were apt to fantasise. I was fond of both of them and knew that if I hadn't played the game, thought Tom was serious and accepted, he would have been horrified and trapped into creating an escape.

Mummy's eightieth birthday arrived; I gave her a simply marvellous party at Fellowship House. There was dancing, cabaret, dinner and later Bridge! She had a rather glamorous boyfriend, Randell, a famous plastic surgeon, much younger than her of course. He was still sewing ears back and reducing bags under eyes. My mother by this time had insisted on having her hip replaced again at the age of seventy-eight because she said the first time they had shortened one of her legs. I told you she was a strong woman, and she put up with another six-hour operation so she could do the first dance with Randell at her party. He would do anything for her, but I know he got nothing in return.

My problems continued one night (or was it morning) Marek, white-faced, sat on my bed and began, "Don't worry, Mummy!" My heart sank, but when I learnt the worse I was very much relieved, as it seems I could very easily have lost my son. He had obliterated our little blue van, having wrapped it around a concrete lamp post. Trying to assert myself (too late), I insisted Marek pay the fifty pounds requested for the post, but later to my utter frustration found that behind my back his grandmother had given him the amount and more, which she eventually, as Marek's behaviour deteriorated, demanded back from me. Not for one moment do I blame Marek. It was my fault. I neglected them both when they needed support far more than I. At least they have both come through it and I'm so proud of them, and the two daughters-in-law I've acquired are far better than I would have even wished for.

Life certainly was never dull. Ken sometimes lost patience

with me. One particular evening we had had a drink at the Tatton Arms overlooking the River Mersey at the end of Boat Lane, one minute's walk from Holly Bank. Ken got really cross and pulled the engagement ring off my finger and threw it in the river, at exactly the same place as Guy D'eutremont had thrown my first ring. I think that's odd! What was quite funny was that I, being practical, went the next morning to look on the river bank, as I could not believe he could throw it that far. A man inquired what I was doing. After I explained he got a pebble about the same weight and stood where Ken had been and threw his pebble as hard as he could. It landed in the water!

I think it took me till my middle fifties until I began to surface. There were some marvellous occasions. To name a few: Marek and Jackie's wedding, which we held at Fellowship Hall. I had tremendous fun making the wedding cake, and I had never iced one before. Jackie wanted a two-tier cake with white pillars, pink hearts, roses, and a pink ribbon, and a bridal couple on the top. I managed it, although I got rather merry as I kept eating the faulty hearts and drinking sherry. Everyone thought it was beautiful, and no one noticed it was a little like the tower of Pisa. Uncle Ted as usual made an impromptu speech to replace Kazik, and I disappeared into the kitchen feeling overwhelmed.

Stephen often let me visit him at Cambridge. One time particularly sticks in my mind, an engineer's dinner. The dinner was quite unforgettable, the wines all suited to each dish, then the marvellous port was handed round. I sat next to a boy whose name was Leeky; I think he was Professor Leeky's son. He reminded me of that actor in *To the Manor Born*. We all ended up in the famous Cellar Bar and danced and danced (as I told you before, something I missed out on). Stephen and his friends were amused because they said as the night progressed and Leeky got drunker, he was under the impression I got younger. Maybe I did

I so enjoyed myself, but hopefully behaved myself too. Another time when I visited we had a Christmas dinner, and hundreds of Christmas puddings came up from the floor all alight on a sort of lift. I had acquired a tiny M.G. Midget for the large sum of one hundred and fifty pounds and passed my test at forty-eight.

GNT 428D (my favourite drink)

One amusing episode was when Ken arranged a surprise sixtieth birthday for me, my God! As you can see time was racing along. I don't think I like surprises, but he had tried his best, and with the help of the boys, everyone turned up to the Italian restaurant in Poynton. It wasn't till halfway through the fun my friend calculated that I was only fifty-nine!

Mummy was becoming more reliant on me. I was not only taking her to her various Bridge engagements and waiting on when her friends played at her house, but I had had a difficult time arranging a ninety percent grant to improve her house. It was arranged that I would paint the interior for five hundred pounds, which was a lot of money, but it was also a lot of work, entailing four rooms and the landing and bathroom. After my efforts I didn't get the money. My mother made some arrangement with her solicitor that everything she spent on improvements went to me when she died. One afternoon she invited the solicitor to come to talk over her will, which was when I learnt the awful truth. The solicitor asked me to leave the room, as I was not included in my father's will. Any money was to go to my sons. I was very hurt. Luckily Maureen was able to arrange that I was not left out, but it still upset me.

Maybe this instigated me to sell up and buy my tiny cottage in the hills above Conwy, not far from Betws-y-Coed where Daddy had stayed with relatives while at Stony Hurst. I would stay a week in the cottage, then go and get Mummy and bring her back to stay for a week. This went on for quite a while.

Just before I moved Stephen gave me a box of oil paints. Mummy and I went to Dunham Massey, where I painted a picture of the garden. As it was my first effort in oil, I prepared to throw it on the fire when my mother said, "Don't do that, it's not bad!" Later on my friends Phillip and Yvonne made me have an exhibition in a studio they owned in Chorlton. I finished and framed seventy paintings and sold nearly all of them. The first one I nearly threw away I sold for one hundred and fifty pounds. In fact I was getting quite a few commissions around the area, but this was all forgotten when I was in the throes of moving. I find that North Wales is full of artists so I have been keeping a low profile. I've been too busy anyway.

Stephen and Gillian asked me to stay with them for a week's rest. I was to drive Mummy to the farm at Carmarthen, where she was to stay with Maureen and Rowland. All went well. We arrived safely and I was to set off the next day, but after breakfast at 9 a.m. I remember washing the dishes and no more until I came to in the garden at about six p.m. with Maureen offering me a cup of tea! I think I screamed for a few seconds, as nine hours were a complete blank! Very unpleasant. All Maureen could explain was that I seemed distressed and disorientated. She rang Stephen and it was arranged they would put me on the bus the next day; Steve and Gill would meet me and take me straight to the doctor. I did feel really odd, hesitant and unable to speak easily. Stephen took me straight to their doctor. All I was told was I was just to rest.

I was determined to have a good time, and as it had been arranged before I became peculiar, we all set off in a party of about six to a beer festival. It was great, and I, determined to prove I was all right, insisted on ordering a round of beers. I got in an awful mess; the beers all have unusual names. For obvious reasons I cannot now remember the exact list, but to give you some idea it went something like this: two One-Night Stands, one Old Peculiar, two Directors and one Old Lizzy! I think eventually Gillian had to help me. I really cannot remember when and how I got back or when I got my car.

My doctor gave my attack a name and reassured me I could drive as soon as I felt able. So back I came to square one: a week alone in my idyllic cottage, then off to Northenden to pick up my mother and bring her to me for a week, or sometimes I stayed with her for a change. Eventually, even with the excellent home help and the added help of Kitty Pomfret, I was unable to leave my mother, so she came to live with me. She paid for an extra bedroom to be added on to the cottage as she was unable to climb the stairs.

She was an amazing woman, which no one can deny. She was not only beautiful, but talented, bright and never boring. She reached the age of ninety-four, but in the last year a woman came from Social Services. That was a strange day. A woman arrived and ordered me to go and find a home for my mother while she stayed with her! I did find a lovely place where she was able to watch the promenade on the West Shore. But once again she spent as many nights as possible with me. Things were difficult. That wheelchair got heavier and heavier as I pushed it into my tiny boot.

One day we went and sat outside the hotel on the West Shore, when to my surprise Mummy ordered a large whiskey (she was not a drinker). I joined her and we sat happily in the sunshine reminiscing. She came home with me but said she would go back to the home to sleep. The next morning they phoned to say she had died. I felt so sad that I had not been with her. I think she would have approved of the funeral, as it was a happy funeral. Friends came, and Maureen, Rowland, Shirley and of course my boys with Jackie and Gillian, who supported and helped, Gillian with a small bump (my first grandchild). We all managed to have tea and of course wine out in the garden. The next day just the family went up the mountain and had a picnic.

Now what? It was strange I no longer had anyone to look after. I felt restless, so for some reason I went to college and took a language course in French. I've never enjoyed myself so much, although it was difficult owing to my lack of education. I did not understand when the tutor referred to such things as verbs, first persons and paragraphs, etc. We often paired off, my partner being a twenty-year-old girl who was doing the course because she was going out to Paris to work as a hairdresser. We really had fun and to my amazement I passed! To celebrate we all had a French meal.

After this I passed my O and A Level in English Literature. To celebrate I decided to go to London to see the Picasso and Matisse exhibition at the Tate Modern. Stephen suggested I went on to Oxshott and spent the weekend with them; he suggested they might celebrate my achievement, but as always things did not go smoothly.

It was one of the warmest days we had; I arrived at Euston hot and irritable, as the air conditioning on the train did not work. We were packed like sardines, for some reason the toilets stank, and as we were in a modern conveyance we could not open the windows. The journey was literally horrendous. Using my mother's stick (strangely I've been able to do without it since) I stumped down the tube, arrived at Southwark and stumped for a further twenty minutes. I was terribly hot and uncomfortable and even considered walking without my shoes. On the way I was lured into a pub. Everyone was sitting outside so I decided to have a shandy.

I eventually arrived at that dreadful interminable concrete slope leading down to the Tate, only to see at the entrance the sign: "NO TICKETS AVAILABLE." When I saw all the Italians and Americans clamouring to no avail I decided as I had come to celebrate I would go up to the best restaurant and have prawns and wine! On the way up on those long escalators I noticed a huge queue waiting at the Picasso and Matisse exhibition. I inquired from someone what they were doing and got the answer, "They've got their ten-pound tickets but they still have to queue for hours because only so many are let in at a time."

I got my prawns and wine and the waiter inquired whether I had seen the exhibition, and I explained, saying I was not pleased. On my way out a smart, handsome young Italian approached me. I can only think he was something to do with the restaurant. He was young but had an air of authority. He said, "Please come with me." We went in a lift past the queue and straight into the exhibition, where this strange young man handed me my ticket. I, rather embarrassed, asked could I pay him. His answer was, "Just go in and enjoy yourself." I gave him a hug, which he returned, and I wandered through the rooms astonished and pleased. So you see life continues to surprise and excite.

My story has now made a full circle and I've reached the age of seventy-eight, but don't think that life is slowing down; if anything it's becoming more interesting, more exciting, and certainly more enjoyable.

A few months ago three girls from the Anglo-Polish Ballet came into my life again! Elizabeth Gammond, Marianne Balchin and Nellie Jean Perkins. We hadn't been in touch for about fifty-nine years, since we were nineteen. It so happened that an artist friend of mine called Elian McCready, while giving a talk on tapestry, mentioned my name. Elizabeth, who was there, said there can be only one Meeta and got my phone number. Since then we've met. Elizabeth lives in Guildford, only a few minutes away from Gillian and Stephen.

Stephen took a photo of us together, amusing because we were both dressed alike in long, to-the-ankle denim skirts and cream blouses! We both realised we would still have recognised each other. And now I'm to stay with Elizabeth next week and go to a reunion for the Anglo-Polish Ballet at the Festival Hall London.

Spring is coming, the daffodils and primroses are awake and flowering and I can sit in my arbour again and raise my glass of Chablis to you all and to the future. I'm thinking of taking a degree, or on the other hand maybe I'll....

THE BEGINNING!

Me in the arbour

Printed in the United Kingdom
by Lightning Source UK Ltd.
110018UKS00001B/99

9 781424 113507